SCRAMBLES
IN THE LAKE DISTRICT

Volume 2: North

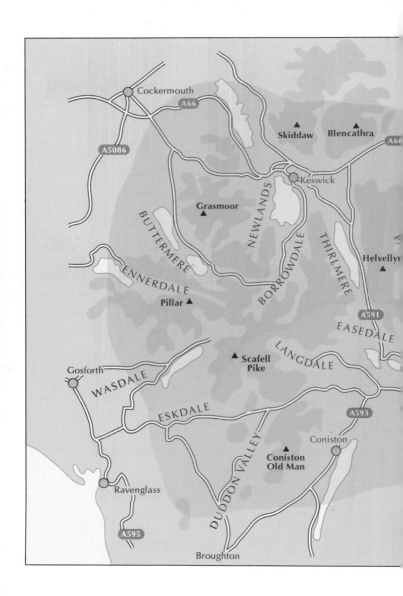

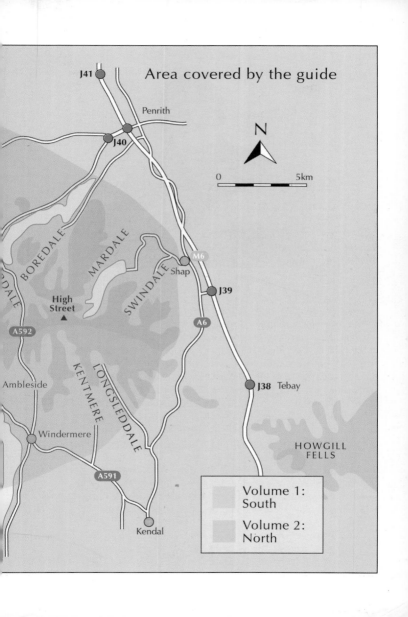

About the Author

Brian Evans, now retired after a career in printing and publishing, has enjoyed a lifetime's love of the outdoors. He has climbed, walked, skied and camped in many parts of Europe and North America, yet always returns to the Lake District, which has a special place in his affections. He prefers to explore out-of-the-way places, preferably with the added attraction of rock, to which he has been addicted since childhood.

Brian has always enjoyed adventure sports including pot-holing, wild-water canoeing, skiing and alpine mountaineering. He still particularly enjoys rock climbing in all its forms, from long adventurous climbs where route-finding skills are necessary to single-pitch bolted sports climbs in the Mediterranean sun. Recently, with encouragement from his grandson, he has taken up mountain biking.

Some of Brian's most memorable trips include multi-day alpine climbs such as the West face routes of the Dru and the Aiguille Noire; walking across the remote interior of Iceland; ski-backpacking in France; canoeing tumultuous alpine rivers; and delving deep underground in the Vercors pot-holes.

At home in Lancashire with his wife, Aileen, and collie, Meg, he enjoys drawing and painting, and planning the next adventurous trip.

SCRAMBLES
IN THE LAKE DISTRICT
Volume 2: North

by
R. Brian Evans

2 POLICE SQUARE, MILNTHORPE, CUMBRIA LA7 7PY
www.cicerone.co.uk

© Brian Evans 2005
© Photos Brian and Aileen Evans, unless otherwise stated
ISBN 185284 463 9

Previously published in 2 vols:

Scrambles in the Lake District
© Brian Evans
First published 1982
Reprinted 1982, 1983
Revised 1985
Reprinted 1988, 1991, 1994,
1996, 1998, 2002
ISBN 0902 363 39 5

More Scrambles in the Lake District
© Brian Evans
First published 1990
Reprinted 1994, 1999
ISBN 1 85284 042 0

Cover: Old West Route, Pillar Rock (Route 27)

CONTENTS

Key to maps and route diagrams

————	scramble route
·············	walk between scramble section
————	approach
– – – – –	variant
·············	hidden route
·············	other useful paths
→	route direction
❶	route number
〰〰〰	road
▲	summit cairn
⅄	col
⬭	water
〰〰	river
⚕	campsite
♣	wooded area
Ⓟ	parking
■	habitation

PREFACE

The first volume of *Scrambles in the Lake District* (1982) brought an enthusiastic response. The book was aimed at those with some experience of climbing and mountaineering and it opened the eyes of many people to the adventurous possibilities that exist in the Lake District. Rock climbers found that scrambling allowed them to salvage something out of a poor day, and the routes were sometimes more than enough to set the adrenalin flowing. Other people found that scrambling changed their concept of a day's fell walking. The second volume, *More Scrambles in the Lake District*, which followed in 1990 also included many memorable routes.

This new edition combines the two books into *Volume 1: South* and *Volume 2: North*. Some new routes are included, some of the less popular discarded, whilst the addition of an extra grade 4 helps to distinguish the more extreme routes.

ACKNOWLEDGEMENTS

My thanks are due to all those people who told me about their favourite scrambles. Special thanks go to Lake District artist Jim Riley, whose fell wanderings are rarely straightforward; if there is rock around, Jim has climbed it. Geoff Dewitt also deserves particular thanks. After enjoying most of the routes in the first *Scrambles* guide, Geoff and his companions Maurice Tedd and Dick Hogg embarked on a systematic appraisal of other scrambling possibilities in the Lake District. Geoff's notes, comments and photographs have proved an invaluable aid in the production of this and earlier guides. All my scrambling companions have contributed to the books, especially John Riding and the late Albert Riding, but most of all my wife Aileen. Her patience and help with the photography have been outstanding. Harry Griffin's books have been an inspiration, particularly his *Adventuring in Lakeland*, which briefly mentions many of the routes in this guide. Peter Davies of the Cumbria Raptor Study Group and Karen Slater of English Nature have both helped in bringing attention to conservation and environmental issues in this latest edition.

Brian Evans

In the upper part of Mosedale Force, Swindale (Route 110)

Scrambling is a popular and rewarding pastime if the following safety code is adhered to. If the code is ignored then you could get into dangerous and possibly lethal situations: unroped scrambling in exposed situations is one of the most dangerous mountaineering practices.

- **Unroped scramblers must not slip!** Take care always to have a good hand-hold or foot-hold. Take care that your hand-hold is sound.
- **An easy, adventurous scramble in dry conditions can be transformed in wet or damp conditions into a potentially lethal misadventure**. Retreat before conditions or difficulties render the trip too hazardous.
- **Keep well within your limits**. Do not ascend where you may be unable to descend. On craglets interspersed with steep grass it is easy for the inexperienced to push into a situation where ascent is dangerous and retreat frightening.
- **A safety rope MUST be carried in the party**. This may be used to safeguard anyone who needs assurance and could be used to rescue anyone in difficulties or off-route.
- **The only relatively safe way to do an exposed grade 2, 3 or 4 scramble is as a roped climb, using belays and running belays**. Unroped scrambling on grade 2, 3 or 4 routes is only for the experienced climber/scrambler.
- **Learn how to use your rope and belays.**
- **Use a helmet when necessary.**
- **In gills expect the holds to be slippery**. Use socks over your footwear to get a better grip. Ensure that your holds are adequate to combat the slippery rock.
- **Think twice before taking children on scrambles**. They often possess neither fear nor judgement. They should be roped at all times and there should be a ratio of two adults to one child.
- **Make sure everyone** in a scrambling party **is aware of the dangers**.
- **Do not underestimate the seriousness of scrambling.**
- **Be aware of conservation issues** and do your best to minimise your impact on the environment.
- **A safe scrambler is someone with a background of mountaineering experience who can cope with rock-climbing situations, loose or slippery rock, has a cautious approach and is not afraid of deciding that conditions render an expedition unsafe.**
- **Please read and heed the introductory notes in guidebooks.** They are the product of experience.

The pinnacle on Chockstone Ridge, Grey Crag, Birkness Combe (Route 39)

INTRODUCTION

The sport of scrambling is not new. The ascent of easy rocks where hands may be used is naturally satisfying and has always been enjoyed by mountaineers, in fact the ascent of the majority of Alpine peaks by their normal route involves some scrambling. Many of the Lake District scrambles have been known since Victorian times and many have been used by generations of climbers. Early climbers created routes that involved roped scrambling without today's numerous aids to safety; high-standard rock climbing has now become so specialized that it is a sport far removed from the rock climbing of even 20 or 30 years ago, and low standard or scrambling routes are no longer relevant in a climber's guidebook full of extremes.

It is difficult to know just where to draw the line and recognise where scrambling becomes rock climbing. Some consider scrambling ends when you need a rope, but this is so much a personal choice that one person's easy scramble is another's frightening climb. I regard scrambling to be an ascent of rock where the hands are necessary for progress, usually with comforting holds. There may also be a few difficult rock moves required in order to overcome an obstacle, but scrambling means never climbing up what you can't climb down. Scramblers also need to take responsibility for their own safety and for their actions on potentially dangerous terrain, a quite different frame of mind from the modern rock climber who may yet feel exposed when venturing a few feet above a bolt or nut protection.

The Lake District scrambles use what the area has to offer and cannot compare with the extensive scrambling available in Skye or other craggier areas, so climbers expecting long, continuous rock routes may be disappointed. Do not expect rock climbs, more a series of rock incidents in a day on the hills. Much is left to the individual – on many of the routes it is a simple matter to bypass most of the rock and reduce the outing to a steep walk. You can also often choose to make the route more difficult by seeking steeper rock problems. I have described in this guide what I consider to be an interesting line, which if lost need not be a calamity, for you may find an equally worthy way.

DANGERS

Scrambling is an adventure sport, which implies that it is dangerous. Part of the attraction of any adventure sport

On the perched block at the top of Harrow Buttress, Grey Crag (Route 39)

lies in safely overcoming potential hazards, and when scrambling this means not slipping. Unlike modern rock climbing, which is steep and generally well protected, a fall whilst scrambling, which is generally unprotected, can be very serious. You must return to the maxim followed by rock climbers before the advent of modern gear – **YOU MUST NOT SLIP**.

Scrambling involves ascending rock that is not usually of sustained difficulty nor steep enough to warrant the use of what are termed 'rock-climbing' skills. However, a word of warning: although, with care, the easier scrambles are quite within the capabilities of a wide range of people, it is worth remembering that **unroped scrambling in exposed situations is potentially the most dangerous of all mountaineering situations**.

On the more difficult scrambles the exposure is often dramatic, and it is advisable to take a rope for safety. Persons tackling these should have experience of rock climbing and the necessary belay and rope techniques to allow a safe ascent or retreat. Good judgement is needed to attempt the routes in bad weather, but an experienced climber should know just how far he or she can go on wet or greasy rock and know when to retreat. **Adventurous walkers who are using this book should tackle the easiest routes only in good conditions**. It is inadvisable to venture on them at all in wintry conditions, as a thin coating of ice over the easiest rocks can create an impossible and dangerous hazard. Snow and ice will turn most of the routes into serious and difficult winter climbs.

The rewards are great and the penalties severe. A recommended book, which delves into the philosophy of the subject, is Colin Mortlock's *The Adventure Alternative* (Cicerone Press). Mortlock has many thought-provoking theories and divides adventure into bands. Every individual has their adventure threshold, the boundary between intense enjoyment and command of the situation, and fear that could result in misadventure. For some individuals that threshold is quite low; others need a much more gripping situation to savour the adventure. Find your threshold and keep within your own limits.

Finally, **think twice before taking children on scrambles**. Whilst they are often natural scramblers and show little fear, they do not possess experience or sound judgement. They need constant supervision and should be roped at all times. Also, leave your dog below for the duration of the trip. Whilst it is possible to push and pull a dog up the easiest gills, it is not fair on you or it. If left to run loose, it will run round the hazards often seeking an escape up loose and vegetated side walls, sending rocks down on the party and doing damage to the environment.

To sum up, the safest scrambler is someone with a background of many years experience of mountaineering, who can cope with rock climbing situations, loose or slippery rock, has a cautious approach and is not afraid of deciding that conditions render an expedition unsafe.

The British Mountaineering Council's participation statement should be heeded.

'The BMC recognises that climbing, hillwalking and mountaineering are activities with a danger of personal injury or death. Participants in these activities should be aware of and accept these risks and be responsible for their own actions and involvement.'

Scrambling on Bell Rib, Yewbarrow (Route 6)

EQUIPMENT AND ROPE TECHNIQUES

When scrambling, it is recommended that you carry a rucksack, complete with all that you deem necessary – a compass, torch, some lunch, your waterproofs and a spare pair of dry socks (to put on after a gill scramble) – especially as most scrambles will be incorporated into a longer walk or a combination of scrambles. In addition, useful maps for the Lake District are the OS 1:25,000 Explorer Series, nos. OL4, OL5, OL6 and OL7. Harvey's Superwalker maps give a clearer, simpler picture of the terrain.

Comprehensive guidance on scrambling equipment and techniques can be found in *The Hillwalker's Guide to Mountaineering* by Terry Adby and Stuart Johnston (Cicerone Press). The following notes are derived from my own experience and are relevant to the particular situations encountered in the Lake District.

Useful websites are: **www.ami.org.uk** (the Association of Mountaineering Instructors) and **www.bmg.org.uk** (British Mountain Guides). Scrambling courses are often available at the National Mountain Centres of Plas y Brenin, **www.pyb.co.uk**, and Glenmore Lodge, **www.glenmorelodge.org.uk.**

Ropes, rope work and belays

Although most scrambling is done unroped, a rope should be carried by the party and must be used when the leader deems that the less confident needs assurance, when the route is extremely exposed (as on an open crag) or to protect a particularly difficult pitch. I use a rope that is 50m long and 9mm thick, which can be used double for short difficulties or single to protect less confident followers. For the grade 4 routes a double rope should be used, as in standard climbing practice. A thicker single rope may be preferred. You must allow a reasonable length of rope for abseiling out of difficulty.

The rope is of little use unless the party can be safely belayed to a firm anchorage. Modern safety techniques are not the prerogative of the climber, and the scrambler must learn the basics. To keep equipment to a minimum I prefer to tie directly to the rope with a bowline or figure-of-eight and use a waist belay; others may

A rope can be reassuring

prefer the comfort of a harness. Trees or spikes may be used as anchors, but more often these are lacking and a nut belay must be inserted into a crack of a suitable width. To this end a selection of three or four varying sized nuts, tape slings and karabiners (including screwgate karabiners for belaying) should be carried in the party. One of the slings should be a long tape that can also serve as an abseil sit-sling. There is no need to clutter oneself with the excessive hardware commonly used in modern rock climbing.

Needless to say, anyone unfamiliar with the techniques required to use this equipment must study a basic rock-climbing instruction book and practice. However, do not be put off – the placement of a firm belay is largely a matter of common sense and the rope handling requirements are quickly learned. The best way of learning is either from an experienced friend or a qualified mountain guide or instructor.

If the leader is highly competent and will not fall, the rope is there to stop the slips of less confident members of the party. Remember, a scrambling slip is more likely to result in a fall over easy-angled or broken

Socks worn over footwear provide a better grip in slippery gills

rock than the steep free-falls of genuine rock climbing, and this means scramblers' falls are more likely to result in injury than a climber falling off a steep crag.

Helmets

Wearing a helmet is undoubtedly safer but many people accept the risk and go without one. However, modern helmets are so light that there is no reason to avoid using one. If a rope is used, again take care that it does not flick any loose stones onto those below.

Footwear

Scrambling is usually done in boots or all-terrain footwear that have a semi-stiff sole and narrow welt. The best have some lateral rigidity in the sole – good quality approach shoes are a popular choice. Avoid dangerous, cheap bendy boots sold in many non-specialist shops and instead choose your boots carefully; secure footwear is a vital safety factor. It may be tempting to use specialist rock boots, but smooth soles are dangerous on grass, which is often encountered on a scramble. Socks (preferably old woollen ones) over the top of approach shoes can be useful in certain circumstances, particularly in a greasy gill. Trainers are not recommended although some people find it easier to take socks over the top of them than boots. If this is the case, trainers should be used as an additional aid and not as a substitute for boots.

First aid kit

Someone in the party should carry and know how to use a first aid kit in order to deal with any minor injury. In case of major accidents that require assistance from Mountain Rescue, use the nearest telephone or a mobile (if there is an adequate signal). Dial 999 and ask for the police.

Foot-holds

When scrambling the most basic requirement is to ascend rock without either slipping or pulling the holds away. In the gills slippery rock is a natural hazard, varying in degree according to location. Always expect your foot to slip if placed on a sloping hold, so ensure that your hand-holds are sufficient that you can regain control if you do slip. In these slippery gill beds, place the boot between rocks so that the boot will tighten its hold if it slips. Use sharp-edged foot-holds, even if they are smaller than more obvious slippery sloping ones. If the pitch is obviously slippery then either take boots off and proceed in socks, or put socks over trainers brought specifically for the purpose (remember that trainers are bendier than boots and will not be as secure on small holds). Be aware that socks wear through!

Easy-angled waterslides pose few problems to climbers used to balance climbing, which relies on foot-holds, with hands low to assist balance. Novice climbers tend to reach ever higher for non-existent jug hand-holds, which makes a slip more probable as the weight of the body is transferred from a vertical position (which helps to hold the foot in place) to a position almost parallel to the slabs (which helps to push the foot off the hold). A slip on a waterslide slab can result in a long and dangerous slide and people below can be swept off like skittles.

Hand-holds

Pulling holds away is easier than you may think, particularly in gills with loose rock or on a fault line where the basic rock structure may be shattered. If there is any possibility that a flake fingerhold may ping off, use it with caution and delicacy. Spikes may be large but insecure. Treat them with respect. Even on the best rock there are loose holds and perched blocks. Aim to avoid a sudden upset of balance. A heave and pull approach can be positively dangerous, particularly if the person is unaware of the dangers. Do not pull outwards on any hold where there is the possibility that it may become detached. Upward progress can often be made more safely by pushing rather than pulling. Knees can be useful.

Roped scrambling

In gills a short rope is necessary to safeguard occasional steep or exposed passages. Most of the scrambling will be done unroped.

On buttresses or craglets, the scrambling is much more open and exposed, route finding is important and

Scrambling on the rough slabs of Grey Knotts (Route 37)

Exposure is high in the slabby corner of Slab and Notch, Pillar Rock (Route 25)

it is easy for the inexperienced to find themselves in a situation where ascent is dangerous and retreat frightening. In these situations roped scrambling is the only relatively safe solution, coupled with sound belaying techniques. Unroped scrambling on grade 2, 3 or 4 routes is only for the very experienced climber/scrambler.

Solo scrambling

Many competent mountaineers enjoy solo scrambling, yet the dangers are many. It is so easy to stray into unforeseen difficulties where retreat is hazardous, especially if the rock is slippery. In a party someone can usually bypass the difficulty and drop a rope; alone any mistake could be costly, and a minor incident may become a major problem. Think twice about going alone – it's much more fun anyway with a companion.

Crag scrambling

Some of the best scrambles in the Lake District are found on crags that are at too easy an angle or are too broken for difficult rock climbing. For scramblers, however, there is a satisfaction about weaving an intricate way up a broken buttress, searching out the most continuous rock to give a long scramble to often end close to a summit. Experienced climbers will find the crags – or craglets – entertaining. In practice, this often means linking suitable outcrops of rock to form a way up the hillside. Alternatively the route takes an easy way through areas of steeper crag. This type of scramble is very exposed and failure to find the correct route could be disastrous. Remember: great care is necessary to avoid a slip, and on many routes (grade 2/3/4), roped scrambling is the safest means of progression.

21

Slabs need balance climbing, with hands low

Gill scrambling

A dry spell, with a low water flow, is the best time for gill scrambling. There are few route-finding problems on gill scrambles; the pitches are often short and there is much less exposure than on crags. Therefore easier gills form a good introduction to scrambling. The Lake District is fortunate in possessing a wealth of gills which give good sport. In years of adventuring in many parts of Europe and Britain I have rarely encountered any counterparts as good as the Lakeland gills.

Gill scrambling demands self-imposed rules for maximum enjoyment. Harry Griffin has described his rules in *Adventuring in Lakeland* (Robert Hale). Basically, rule one is to take the hardest route and that closest to the water, only straying from the streambed when the direct way is impassable. Rule two is to stick to the rock as much as possible, only wading – or in extreme cases, swimming – when progress by climbing is impossible. This often means performing difficult rock moves a few centimetres above a pool, or struggling to ascend a difficulty when it would be much easier to walk round. Griffin advocates a direct approach despite waterfalls and spray and even scorns the idea of doing the gills in drought. I prefer to assume that my legs will get wet but draw the line at anything else, and the gills are described here on that basis. However, water conditions are so variable that each party will probably encounter slightly different problems and have to make their own judgements.

The most serious gill scrambles, some would say the only ones worth doing, lie in ravines, which are common in the Lake District, but having sampled the delights of the clean water-washed rock, more open streams are not to be dismissed. Gills which cascade over broad belts of rock give entertaining scrambling with a choice of route and opportunity to make the ascent as difficult or as easy as you wish. Nevertheless, a rope should be carried to safeguard the occasional hazard and provide protection for anyone in the party who requires it.

Bear in mind that some of the gills are heavily vegetated and can be oppressively luxuriant in the height of summer. Midges can also prove troublesome at times. Choosing the right gill for the available conditions needs thought. When Lakeland is

Keep to the rocky bed of the gill to avoid damaging rare vegetation
Sourmilk Gill, Borrowdale (Route 52)

23

Traversing above a deep pool is a feature of gill climbing
Sourmilk Gill, Borrowdale (Route 52)

blighted by a pall of low-lying unmoving cloud which renders crags slippery and hillwalking unattractive, gills can be entertaining and rewarding, provided there is not too much water flowing. In a prolonged dry spell, go for those special routes which rarely come into perfect condition. These routes are in gills that normally carry a good deal of water and drain a large area. The small gills are feasible after a few days of dry weather in summer. In a period of mixed weather, when the ground remains sodden, you may find more water than you anticipated. A good gill

scramble can be rendered useless if you cannot easily criss-cross the stream and use water-washed rock. Spring brings other problems. I have been thwarted, on a perfect day in a dry spell, by snow meltwater.

A dry spell in winter can give good gill scrambling, particularly as you are sheltered from the wind, but beware of ice lingering in ravines; water-splashed rock with an almost invisible veneer of ice can be hazardous. In true winter conditions some gills provide magnificent winter-climbing routes, but these are out of the scope of this guide.

by Karen Slater (English Nature)

What are gills?

The term 'gill' is Scandinavian in origin and is generally associated with the Lake District and especially with the Borrowdale volcanic series, where streams exploit its weaknesses. A gill can be a relatively open small stream but usually refers to one with very steep sides and a rocky bed. The alternative spelling of 'ghyll' was coined by the Victorians and is poetic in origin, and its use correlated with the Victorians' increasing interest in and romanticism of the landscape as they took trips to admire the waterfalls within the gills – the previous boardwalk in Tilberthwaite Gill was evidence of this.

Gills are not, however, confined to the Lakes. Gorge scrambling has now extended to north Wales, where it is causing local problems, and many of the upper glens of Scotland (such as Glen Nevis and Glen Etive) have similar characteristics to the gorges of the Lakes. Abroad, similar features are found in western Norway and the Pyrenees, being associated with high humidity, but on a grander scale.

Early climbers

Early climbers originally followed the lines of weakness and naturally scrambled up the gills before gradually turning to climb the steeper gullies. Interest in the gills persisted and in the last 15 years has undergone a renewal of interest. This has been partly because of their aesthetic appeal and the freedom to move without ropes and partly because of their attractiveness for increasing the number of students from outdoor centres who can be taken out with a single instructor. There has been increasing publicity describing scrambles, and although some of these routes are on the cliffs, many of them are also up the gills. Gill scrambling has therefore been with us almost since the start of climbing and people still enjoy this activity. The routes up the gills are used either as a way up to the higher peaks or just for the pleasure of the rocks and as an end in itself.

The appeal of the gills

There is a great **aesthetic appeal** of the contrast between the delicate plants on the one hand and the mountain landscapes on the other. Gills are the relics of the original forest vegetation and are fragments that show what the original landscape would have been before the interference of man. It is very evocative to climb up a gill, even one as popular as Dungeon Gill, and get an impression of what the original landscape would have been like before the arrival of man. However, the gills occupy a very small area and with the precariousness of the plants clinging to the walls they are very fragile and are easily damaged by those climbing up the gill side.

The harm popularity can cause
Scrambling has caused formerly obscure places to suddenly become immensely popular and this can lead to irreversible damage. Carelessness is the main cause of the problems; apart from the damage arising from the trail of open gates, litter and broken walls, people can also harm the soft vegetation on the gill walls. The mountain gills are especially vulnerable because they have developed so far without disturbance. The last ice age left Lakeland some 10,000 years ago and in its wake waves of plants colonised the bare debris left by the retreating ice, eventually leading to rich and complex vegetation.

What vegetation can be found in the gills today?
The first colonisers of the Lake District were alpine plants, which were resistant to cold and exposure. These were eventually replaced over much of the landscape by birch and pine, which in turn gave way to the familiar oak and ash. However, the rocky sides of the gills and the mountain summits always

Groups often use the easier gills

remained clear of trees. The fragments of vegetation are thus similar to the mountains of the continent and the lowlands of the Arctic and Scandinavia. Forest trees filled the valleys and the hillsides up to about 520m before, gradually over the centuries, man cleared the forest and brought sheep to graze on the fells. The only refuges left for the alpine plants remaining were the protected cliffs and rocky gill sides. Such sheltered sites occupy only a tiny fraction of the land surface (less than 0.5%).

The lower part part of Mill Gill has a luxuriant carpet of moss (Route 70)

Today different groups of plants are found within the many gills – their ecological preferences determining which gill offers the best environment for them. In the lower gills there are many woodland species; **oak** and **ash** give way to **birch** and **rowan** at higher levels. Some woodland plants, such as **wood anemone** and **violet**, still manage to grow on the highest cliffs and gills, but the most common plants throughout the gills are the moorland and woodland species. A specialised group of species, including **butterwort** and **devil's-bit scabious**, is also present on ledges beside water trickles. Because of the dampness of the soil and its peaty texture careless feet and hands very easily destroy these ledges. Also growing on some ledges are plants with a preference for richer soils that are usually found in lowland meadows, such as **meadowsweet** and **globeflower**. Finally there are the special alpine species like the mossy **saxifrage** and **roseroot**; these are only found in the higher gills.

The composition of the gills thus changes with altitude as the climate and environment become more severe; here only upland species can survive. Thus only in the high-level gills that are situated 450m up on the side of Helvellyn, the Langdale Pikes and even more famously on the north side of the Scafell range will you find a few **dwarfed rowan** bushes clinging to the cliffs. The highest gill sides are bare of trees and have comparable vegetation to the Arctic.

Which gills in particular are important?
Both the **individual plant species** and **the assemblages** in which they occur are important. Many gills are within Sites of Special Scientific Interest (SSSI). The following gills are notified as SSSIs:

- Stanley Gill
- Dungeon Gill
- Tilberthwaite Gill
- Skelghyll Beck
- Browgill
- Stockdale Becks
- Sourmilk Gill (Buttermere).

There are also gills designated SSSIs that are within wider upland/woodland:

- Thirlmere Woods (Launchy Gill)
- Lodore and Troutdale Woods (including Watendlath Beck and Ashness Gill)
- Scafell Pikes (including Ruddy Gill, Greta Gill and Calf Cove Gill)

- Naddle Forest (including Guerness Gill)
- Helvellyn and Fairfield (including Hogget Gill)
- Great Wood (Cat Gill)

The start of Ruddy Gill (Route 56) where it tumbles into Grains Gill

- Armboth Fells
- Skiddaw group
- Buttermere Fells
- Wasdale Screes
- Pillar and Ennerdale Fells
- Seatoller Woods (Sourmilk Gill)
- Seathwaite Graphite Mine.

A high nature conservation interest is shown in many other gills have that have not been notified as SSSI. Some examples are:

- Sandbed Gill (St Johns in the Vale)
- White Gill near Coniston
- Holbeck Gill, Troutbeck
- Atkinsons Grain near Bampton
- Combe Gill, Rosthwaite
- Middlesteads Gill, Thirlmere
- Crinkle Gill, Langdale
- Raise Gill.

When scrambling up the walls of the gills place your feet and hands carefully, avoiding damaging vegetation or even pulling off branches of trees. These impacts may destroy vegetation that may never regrow in our lifetime.

How can you help?

If we are to conserve the unique and beautiful array of plants in the gills then we have to spread quickly and widely the message that these plants are particularly sensitive to careless use.

Ensure that you

- keep to the rocky bed of the gill
- follow only established routes
- keep groups in line
- avoid crumbling rocks where many of the delicate species lie
- leave the plants for others to enjoy.

If these suggestions are followed much of the sensitive vegetation can be conserved, and we can leave for future generations the attractive plants that we ourselves enjoy today.

Please go to the gills and enjoy them: respect the plants and be aware of the surroundings and the impacts that you can have.

Bad weather scrambling

Many rock climbers use scrambles as a means of salvaging something exciting on a day of poor weather. **However, in bad conditions the crags are treacherously slippery and many climbers have got more than they bargained for. Do not underestimate the seriousness of these routes**. Remember the aspect of a crag is very important: south- and west-facing rocks are usually cleaner and quicker drying. At the onset of rain, before the water has chance to build up flow, the clean water-washed rocks of a gill scramble may still offer good sport.

Exploratory scrambling

Exploratory scrambling can create some interesting and hazardous days. Most people will be content to tackle the standard good quality routes, but for the person who has done everything – that is, most of the rock climbs and scrambles within his/her grade, and most of the popular summits, scrambling where fancy takes you can be quite satisfying. However, a word of warning: if you are not careful you can easily get into some particularly nasty situations. There is an awful lot of rubbishy crag in the Lake District! The best rough rock lies in the central fells, whilst east of Thirlmere it tends to be smoother and more vegetated. The Skiddaw Slates, which comprise all the fells north of Buttermere (except the head of Newlands), are shattered and rarely give good scrambling. One or two gills that seem promising prove slippery and the water-washed channel may be veiled with a curtain of moss (some are good winter

Symbols used in the text are as follows:

⚠ = route within an SSSI (Site of Special Scientific Interest)
❦❦ = gill with great nature conservation interest
❦ = gill with some nature conservation interest.

Grading

Grades are for ascents in good dry conditions. Wet rock, particularly on the crags, can increase the grade considerably or render a scramble extremely hazardous. I have introduced a grade 4 to replace the traditional 3S, which denoted an especially serious route. All scrambling is serious.

Grade 1 is a straightforward scramble, with little or no route-finding difficulty. The described route takes the most interesting line, which can usually be varied or even avoided at will. Generally, the exposure is not great, but even so, great care must be taken to avoid a slip.

Grade 2 contains longer and more difficult stretches of scrambling, and a rope may be useful for ensuring safety in the more exposed passages. Although individual sections of the scramble can usually be avoided, these sections may be inescapable once the scramble is underway. Some skill in route finding is required to follow the described line.

Grade 3 is a more serious proposition, only to be undertaken by competent parties. Escape is difficult. A rope is advisable for safety on exposed passages and for some pitches of easy rock climbing. The routes require a steady leader with the ability to judge how the rest of the party are coping with the situations, and a rope should be used wherever the safety of an individual is in doubt.

Grade 4 denotes a particularly serious outing, perhaps containing very exposed passages on steep rock, poor rock or vegetation. Recommended only for experienced, competent climbers who will almost certainly use a rope on key pitches. Escape is difficult. This supersedes the 3S grade used in previous guides (many of the lower graded routes are still serious propositions).

Note that grade 3 and 4 routes, particularly in gills, may include moves which would merit up to a 'v diff' grading in rock-climbing guides.

Many of the routes described follow what I consider to be the most rewarding route for continuity and interest. This often involves scrambling over rock outcrops, which could be easily avoided by a short detour (thus reducing the grading with the consequent loss of interest). So much is up to the choice of the individual. Rock climbers will doubtless choose their own lines to suit their chosen standard or use the scrambles as a variation of 'bouldering'.

The star system
This gives a useful indication of quality. **One star** (✳) represents a route, which although not classic, has its good points and is worthy of attention. **Two stars** (✳✳) represent a route of more continuous interest and a good line, whilst **three stars** (✳✳✳) are reserved for classic routes with more continuously interesting scrambling that is based on a good line.

ice-climbs but these are of no interest to the scrambler).

The pioneer rock climbers often chose gullies for their climbs, with a mistaken sense of security. I would strongly advise the scrambler to keep away from most gullies, for they are dank and desperate. Invariably the rock is slippery and even the most innocent-looking cleft has its bed blocked by chockstones which are often strenuous and serious obstacles.

Stick to the easy-angled little craglets and string them together to make an interesting ascent, or choose a pleasant open streambed to follow to the tops. Make sure you are not disturbing nesting birds and take great care not to damage the environment.

CONSERVATION AWARENESS

Concern has been expressed by conservationists and botanists that gill scrambling leads to the destruction of a sensitive habitat for rare plants and birds. The conflict of interest between the adventure-seeking scrambler and the conservationists is not an easy one to resolve. Please be aware of the problem and leave no sign of your passage. If you stick to the clean water-washed rock then no damage is inflicted on the vegetation. Once you have recourse to the side walls you could damage the vegetation.

Some of the gills are in protected SSSIs (Site of Special Scientific Interest) and should be traversed with the utmost care. Those routes that are in such areas are identified in the guide as being SSSIs or as areas of nature conservation interest (see Using this Guide, above, for further details).

Do not pollute the stream, it may be someone's water supply, but before taking a drink yourself, remember that ravines are often the last resting place of suicidal sheep! Some crags with nesting peregrines or ravens are subject to access restrictions in the nesting season. Details of these are available on the BMC website: **www.thebmc.co.uk**

THE ROUTES

The scrambles are described valley by valley beginning with Wasdale. The map reference refers to the approximate start of each route. Right and left means in the direction of travel. The height of a route is the vertical height gain and will include a mixture of rock scrambling and walking.

Very few of the routes as described are suitable for descent; but some can be descended close to the described route if you choose easier alternatives on grassy rakes. Generally, an ascent is so much more worthwhile that it is best to plan an itinerary combining several ascents, rather than lose interest in an unsatisfactory descent. When looking up a rocky buttress the continuous scrambling is obvious. When looking down, there often appears to be a surfeit of grass and it is difficult to choose a continuous rock descent.

ACCESS, CONSERVATION AND BIRD RESTRICTIONS

by Kevin Howett and Peter Davies
(Chairman of the Cumbria Raptor Study Group)

Reproduced with permission of the Fell and Rock Climbing Club

Access and conservation

Access to the crags of the Lake District is taken for granted by the majority of visitors but in fact in some cases access may have been achieved only through years of patient negotiation. Fortunately, the **National Trust**, **Forestry Commission**, **United Utilities** and other private owners who are broadly sympathetic to climbers own most of the Lakeland crags. In a few cases, however, the situation remains delicate and increasing numbers of climbers or scramblers are only likely to make it more so. This is an area in which we can all help, not only by cherishing this region in the manner it deserves – parking thoughtfully, co-operating with farmers and landowners, following the country code, observing bird restrictions, picking up litter at crags and so on – but by ensuring that others do the same. Outsiders look on climbers as a group, and inconsiderate behaviour by a few will be seen, rightly or wrongly, as a reflection upon us all. The onus is on all of us to make certain that it doesn't happen in the first place.

Bird restrictions

Several of the Lake District crags carry **bird restrictions** in the spring (typically from 1st March to 30th June). However, the situation changes from year to year and climbers should make efforts beforehand to find out if there are Schedule 1 birds or ravens in residence on the crag they intend to visit. Usually restricted crags will be signed, but this may not always be the case, and all climbers or scramblers should acquaint themselves with the latest known details which can be found on the BMC website at **www.thebmc.co.uk** or on the FRCC website at **www.frcc.co.uk/rock/birds.htm**. Where birds have not nested in any particular year, the ban may be lifted earlier. If there are birds nesting, and there is an agreed restriction, then please be prepared to change your plans according to the agreement. It may be that only some parts of the crag are restricted, so other routes can be climbed. If this is the case it will be indicated on the signs. The notes below have been drawn up jointly by the Lake District National Park Authority, the

National Trust, the Cumbria Raptor Study Group, English Nature, The British Mountaineering Council Area Committee and the Fell and Rock Climbing Club. They are intended to cover only the Lake District and outlying areas of Cumbria, though they may be found useful elsewhere.

All birds and their eggs and nests are protected by the **Wildlife and Countryside Act 1981**. Certain rare or more endangered species are further protected by increased penalties under the 1981 act and must not be intentionally or recklessly disturbed when nesting. These birds are listed in the act and are referred to as Schedule 1 species. Many are ground-nesting or tree-nesting birds, some are found on sea cliffs, but the Schedule 1 bird species that climbers may most commonly encounter on crags in the Lake District is the peregrine falcon. Some agreed restrictions also apply to ravens (though these are not Schedule 1).

Peregrines
Peregrines are the largest falcons in the British Isles. They can be recognized by their distinctive profile, often sighted from the crag, as they plummet groundwards to seize some unsuspecting prey. Seen from below, they are pale-coloured birds with dark tips to the tail and wings. Their call is a piercing shriek, once heard never forgotten, particularly if you are leading at the time! When the peregrine is disturbed this is uttered repeatedly for long periods. Peregrines hunt over a variety of habitats catching medium-sized birds, mainly feral pigeons, by swooping at speeds of up to 200km an hour to seize them. The optimum and preferred nesting sites of peregrines in the United Kingdom are rocky coastal areas, cliffs and inland crags, but the actual nest site is not at all obvious, being just a shallow scrape in the soil. Some indication may be given by streaks of white guano (bird droppings) down an area of the crag, though this may merely be a roost site for the male rather than a nest.

Peregrines are fairly common in the Lake District which is one of their most important European habitats, but they are rare elsewhere. In fact the United Kingdom supports approximately 14% of the European population. Of these, in Cumbria, there are usually about 85 nesting sites which hold one or more birds each year and approximately 65 pairs attempt to breed each season. This is 6% of the UK's total population and is considered to be the densest breeding population in the world. The Cumbrian birds are especially important because of the population numbers and productivity which is enabling the birds to spread and re-colonise other areas in the UK. They are particularly vulnerable to the weather, disturbance, poor food supply and illegal activities such as shooting, poisoning, and egg and chick theft. In 2000 there were 83 occupied territories on which 46 pairs reared 111 young. However, in 2002 only 32 young were reared and this was the worst recorded breeding season for 30 years, predominantly due to appalling weather, but also to increased robberies. Climbers can assist here by reporting any suspicious characters they see near peregrine nest sites.

Ravens
Ravens are very large black birds, similar to a rook but a third bigger. They have distinctive deep 'pruk-pruk' and 'grok' calls and are great aerial acrobats that delight in soaring and tumbling. Ravens, while not protected in the same way as peregrines and eagles, are still under potential threat from increased disturbance, and there are some voluntary restrictions in the Lake District on their account. Their nests are very large piles of twigs.

Bird Restrictions Agreements
Bird Restrictions are agreed annually between the local BMC Area Committee, the National Park Authority and English Nature. The area of crag agreed to be avoided can vary depending upon various factors including the layout of the crag. Some pairs also vary their choice of nesting site each year either within a crag or between different crags and so agreements may change from year to year. In general, they only apply to the most popular rock-climbing crags but this does not mean that people are necessarily allowed to climb or scramble on all other crags during this period; even where a crag is not subject to a restriction, if you suspect a bird (particularly a peregrine) is nesting on it, you should heed the advice below. Areas where birds are known to nest should be avoided for a period running from the 1st March to 30th June in the case of the peregrine, and from 1st March to 31st May for the raven.

How the law affects you
The law states that it is an offence to 'intentionally' or 'recklessly' disturb a Schedule 1 bird 'at, on or near' the nest. It is also an offence to recklessly or intentionally disturb 'dependent' fledged young. These fledglings are young birds that have just moved away from the nest but are still dependent to some extent on their parents for food and protection.

It is clear and unambiguous what 'at' and 'on' mean in this legislation, but the law does not stipulate a definition for 'near'. Nor does the law stipulate what constitutes 'disturbance'. It would be difficult to do this, as each bird species is different, and indeed individual birds are different. As a result, the prosecution would call upon expert witnesses to testify that disturbance occurred. It would also have to be shown that it was intentional or reckless.

Many peregrine falcon sites are monitored under licence by **Raptor Study Groups**, and it is important that scramblers follow some basic guidance in order to minimise disturbance (and allow both birds and scramblers to continue to coexist) as well as to make sure they are not breaking the law. Apart from possible prosecution, if you are arrested police can confiscate your climbing equipment as evidence to present at the trial, and the case may take a long time to come to court.

The following information will give a basic knowledge of Schedule 1 bird behaviour for scramblers to judge for themselves what action to take. It is not intended to be definitive, but to be a general guide.

At the crag

If you visit a crag not listed as having an agreement, but then notice activity from a peregrine or other Schedule 1 bird in the vicinity, then the guidance below will help you decide what to do. It can equally be used for some other nesting birds you may come across, such as ravens. Obviously, your choice of what can be done will depend on the extent of the crag and its topography as well as other factors outlined below.

The prow of Bell Rib (Route 6)

The exposed crossing of Glaciated Slab on Intake Ridge (Route 60)

As you walk into the crag keep a look out for peregrines and other birds. Peregrines in particular may be calling as they fly about the area. When you arrive they may be disturbed but this is quite normal intuitive disturbance. Try and move out of their line of sight as quickly as you can and then wait and see if they settle down, and then try to spot where they originate. This will enable you to decide whether there is a nesting site that is being used near the route that you are hoping to do and to assess from the disturbance criteria below whether you feel your presence will be detrimental to the birds.

If the nest site is not directly beside where you are going to climb, if the configuration of the crag means you can be separated from line of sight from the nest site to some extent or if the crucial period of egg incubation (see below) in cold weather is past, you will probably find that the birds will have calmed down after the initial disturbance and that your climbing does not disturb them off the nest for long periods.

If the birds continue to appear aggressive and agitated and are staying away from the nest, you should find another route further away from the site, on another part of the crag, or indeed another crag. To continue climbing could keep the parents off the nest for too long so causing damaging disturbance.

How do you judge disturbance?

Most birds will act instinctively to protect their nest site when they perceive a threat. They will often make an initial reaction to human presence by calling, often repeatedly or aggressively. They will then either realise there is no threat and will settle down or, if they continue and you then move away from them, they will then stop their instinctive behaviour.

It can be difficult for non-ornithologists to judge when a peregrine's call changes from normal activity to that of a protection call, but listen for a more aggressive tone. If the female then flies from the nest and stays away, then they have been disturbed and it becomes detrimental to breeding success.

How close is too close?

There are no hard and fast rules to determine when you might be too close as so much depends upon the tolerance of the individual bird. If the crag is very popular with climbers or scramblers, any nesting birds may be habituated to the presence of climbers. Such peregrines may be able to accept climbing in quite close proximity, as long as it is around the other side of an arête or on a separate buttress. One thing that you can be sure of is that climbing very close or directly onto the nest will cause damaging disturbance. At crags in remote areas where there is little climbing activity birds may be disturbed even at some distance. Of particular importance is the line of sight. If the bird can see you it is far more likely to be disturbed. The best policy is to err upon the side of caution, and if in any doubt retreat.

The most important period of nesting

For most birds the most sensitive periods are up to the time they lay their eggs, and when they have just laid eggs; for peregrines this period can be from February to late April when the ambient air temperature is still low. A later sensitive period is when the chicks have just hatched (for peregrines, mid- to end of May). If adults are repeatedly or continually kept off the nest by climbers the eggs or chicks will quickly cool and die, or become available to predation. Obviously there is an even greater risk in cold conditions, and the position of the nest (on a north- or south-facing crag) and the time of day will also be important factors to take into account. For ravens, the period from mid-April to mid-May when they are feeding their chicks is critical as this process needs to be constant throughout the day or the chicks will starve.

What to do if challenged or arrested

Even with the best of intentions it is possible that, having obeyed the above guidelines, you may be accused of disturbing a bird, or of climbing on a crag where you should not have done. If asked to leave please do so without fuss, but please ask and note the name of the person requesting you to leave, the organisation they represent, and the reason you have been asked to leave. If the worst happens and you are arrested, as soon as possible make full notes of the circumstances leading up to your arrest with especial detail on the position of any nests vis-à-vis your climb and the behaviour of any birds. These notes will form vital evidence if the case goes to court, which may be months or even years after the event. In all circumstances please report the details to the **BMC**.

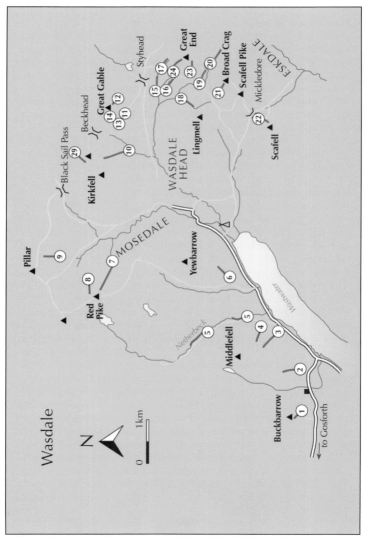

Wasdale

N

0   1km

Buckbarrow
to Gosforth
Middlefell
Netherbeck
Yewbarrow
Westwater
MOSEDALE
Red Pike
Pillar
WASDALE HEAD
Kirkfell
Black Sail Pass
Beckhead
Great Gable
Styhead
Lingmell
Great End
Broad Crag
Scafell Pike
Mickledore
ESKDALE
Scafell

WASDALE

The shapely fells around Wasdale Head are a magnet for walkers, climbers and summer tourists. Wadale Head was the birthplace of Lake District rock climbing, when the Victorian mountaineers based their activities at the inn and pioneered many of the scrambles listed here. There is excellent sport on both high- and low-level crags. Facing The Screes across Wastwater are three beautiful little peaks that repay a visit. These are Buckbarrow, Middlefell and Yewbarrow, which often have better weather than the peaks around the valley head. Surrounding Wasdale Head are the major peaks of Kirkfell, Great Gable and the whole range of Scafell Pikes and Scafell. Mosedale bites deeply in towards Pillar and Red Pike. The classic scramble of Pillar Rock in Ennerdale is most often done from Wasdale.

There are campsites at Santon Bridge, Strands and the National Trust site at Wasdale Head, and a small site at Wasdale Head Inn. The inn also offers bunkhouse accommodation.

Car parking and transport

Even at the busiest times, car parking is easy. There are numerous places alongside the road by Wastwater and a popular parking on the Green, a triangle of common at Wasdale Head. Parking is also available at the National Trust campsite. There is no bus service up the valley.

1. Pike Crag, Buckbarrow

Grade 2✹✹ NY136057

When the high fells are out of condition, the lower rocky hills at the western end of Wasdale provide excellent sport. The south-facing rocks dry quickly, have good friction and form a fine grandstand view from which to enjoy the impressive views over Wastwater to the Screes and Scafell. The crag was first ascended in 1892 by Collie, King and Brunskill.

Rather earthy at the start, the route winds intricately through a steep lower buttress to finish up the crest of an easier ridge. Height gain 110m.

Pike Crag, Buckbarrow

Approach: Buckbarrow overlooks the Gosforth–Wasdale road and cars may be parked by the roadside where it comes nearest the crags at their western end, close to a wall. The buttress to aim for is directly below the summit and to the left of a large scree gully. A direct ascent from the road would be unpleasant and trackless, so it is best to follow a slight path which ascends just to the right of the wall. This is heading for the most popular rock-climbing area. Follow the path well up until a faint track branches across the scree to the right and you gain terraces running horizontally below the broad front of the crags. Traverse these to the right, past a central gully, to the scree gully on the right of the main crag. Ascend to a prominent holly below the start of the rocks proper.

Route: The lower part of the route takes the steep buttress to the left of the ridge, and it is essential to find and follow the correct way. This gives interesting but exposed scrambling. Take the rocks to the right of the holly and aim for a deep cleft which is 6m left of the buttress edge. Step onto a heather ledge 6m below the cleft and cross to an easy-angled mossy rib 9m to the left. The good scrambling starts here. Cross the front of the rib leftwards for 6m to a ledge with perched blocks, then continue up a clean staircase on the right of a mossy slab. Move right under a steep wall then follow a heather rake which leads

The easier upper ridge crest of Pike Crag,
Buckbarrow. Photo: G.Dewitt

leftwards to a large perched block. Squeeze behind this to reach a clean rib 6m to the left. Follow this until easy ledges back on the right gain the edge of the buttress overlooking the gully. The steep initial buttress has been surmounted with surprising ease and the crest of the ridge above is revealed. Scramble up the interesting edge to a grass platform. The step above is taken by an airy gangway close to the edge. A steep tower can be avoided on the left or climbed direct to a ledge below a final steep barrier. Turn this on the left by a gangway which slants back right. Easy scrambling follows to the summit cairn.

Best descent is by a path which goes well to the west to avoid the crags and descends by a stream to gain the road.

MIDDLEFELL

The next of the three low fells presents a jumble of easy-angled crags on its south-east side above Wastwater. There is a great choice of scrambling on good quality rock but beware of occasional loose blocks. The following scrambles are from left to right along the fellside.

2. White Band Crag, Middlefell

Grade 2✻ NY147062

Somewhat mossy rock, but firm and rough with a choice of exposed routes. Height gain 130m.

This route lies well to the left on a prominent white-banded buttress towards the western end of Middlefell, the last notable rocks before Greendale Gill.

Approach: Park below the rocks about half-way between Wastwater and Greendale Farm along the Gosforth road. A bracken-free tongue runs towards the crag, and a slight track on its left edge gains a shelf. Bear right through

White Band Crag, Middlefell

white band

boulders

bracken

bracken to a tree and large boulders. Keep left of the top-most boulder to reach a shoulder beyond, whence a steep rough ascent leads to the first rocks.

Route: Start at the lowest subsidiary rocks at a steep nose with a tree on its right. Climb the left side. Walk to the foot of the main rocks where a central depression with two trees is flanked by ribs. Avoid the steep start of the right-hand rib by a rake on the right-hand side. Easy mossy slabs are then climbed to the 6m-high White Band. Cross this and climb slabs above right of centre, just left of a mossy scoop. Level with a tree on the right, the angle eases. Climb the centre of rough slabs for 20m then take a line diagonally right, crossing below a mossy crack. 6m round the corner climb the front of a rib for 4m then move left 4m into a groove. The easiest line is on the right, linking grassy ledges about 6m left of the right edge to the top of the rock knoll.

Ahead slightly left are more rocks – walk across to the first slabs, gained by a break in the steep left wall. Pleasant scrambling then leads to the top. Other minor outcrops further right can be incorporated on the way to the summit.

Scrambling on White Band Crag, Buckbarrow

If you descend towards Greendale Gill to the west, you will notice two narrow rocky gills on its eastern side – **Tongue Gills**. The left-hand one is a particularly striking rocky rift with thin waterslides, but it is not worth investigating for scrambling.

3. Long Crag and Goat Crag, Middlefell

Grade 1, 2 or 3 NY157063

The next stretch of good scrambling rock lays either side of Goat Gill. Each outcrop, some quite sizeable, can be included or avoided at will,

Approach: Park near the highest point of the road in this area, less than ½ mile south-west of Netherbeck Bridge.

Route: Long Crag has the easier-angled rocks, whilst on the right the described Grade 1 route links the lower Foegill Crags and culminates in the broad buttress of Goat Crag, used as a finish to Route 4.

From the high point of the road, a slight track goes right, under the first rock outcrop which has a pleasant easy-angled rib. The next outcrop above, marked by yew

Whilst the scrambling as a whole is not serious, individual sections may prove to be surprisingly difficult if the easiest line is scorned. Height gain 280m.

Goat Crag, Middlefell

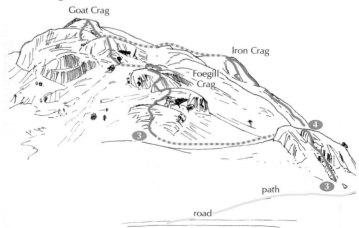

47

Scrambling on the outcrops of Foegill Crags

trees, is a toilsome walk through dense bracken, so include some easy rocks on the left to minimise the struggle. Left of a broad yew is a tempting flaky rib, but this has a very difficult climbing finish. Avoid it by easy rocks on the left side, which curl into walking slabs to reach a gap before the next steep smooth knoll. The easiest way is on the left up rising ledges left to the edge then ascend back right. Harder grade 3 ways climb a thin crack on the right or a diagonal ascent which joins the crack near its top. Two successive small knolls on the right are followed by a steeper buttress with an overhung recess at its foot. Scramble the easy rocks left of the recess to reach a platform below the more continuous rocks of Goat Crag. These offer a long stretch of easy scrambling with plenty of choice.

4. Iron Crag, Middlefell

Grade 1❋ or 3❋ NY156066

The main part of the scramble is on rocks to the right of a shallow stream and scree hollow, directly above Netherbeck Bridge.

Approach: Park by the bridge and walk through bracken close to the slight stream to the lowest rocks on the right.

Route: The first small tier is passed by two small rock steps just right of the stream. Walk through bracken to a steep nose climbed on shelving mossy rock, trending right to avoid the steepest part then back left to a rock crest. Cross a scree patch to another steep nose just on the left. Climb this just left of the edge, then easy rocks follow to the terrace below the main crag. There is a steep continuous buttress on the left, a short steep central block, then easier slabs on the right. The grade 1 continuation takes the right-hand slabs to

Easy but airy scrambling linking as much rock as you like. Rough clean rock, but beware of the occasional perched block. Height gain 250m.

Iron Crag, Middlefell

Goat Crag

Iron Crag

grade 3 var.

a crack with a tree in the short steep wall above. Then walk left to join the crest of the grade 3 route.

The more difficult rock-climbing route takes the challenge of the left-hand buttress and requires some competence in route finding. The situations are exposed, though the holds are generally good. **Rope advised.** A more difficult direct rock climb starts at the same point. Start at a pointed flake at the base of the clean rib. Climb up just left of the rib to an unstable perched flake (do not touch). Come round the front below this using good holds just past it. Move up a step then go right into a groove. Make an awkward prickly exit or, more elegantly, move right along a ledge and up easily to a perch on the crest below a steep wall. Cross right to a ledge, from which two large rock steps lead boldly to easier rocks on the crest and a junction with the grade 1 route.

The scrambling continues on easier-angled rock. When it peters out, further scrambling on the summit crags can be reached by a short walk down to the left to a belt of slabs on the upper section of Goat Crag (Route 3). This is quite nice on the right or longer in the centre. Above are further rock steps to the summit.

✻ ✻ ✻

5. The Netherbeck Gorges

Grade 2✻ NY161070

Two gorges in this gently rising valley are of spectacular beauty. Trees almost form a canopy over the gorges and few walkers realise that just below the path is a deep vertical gash with cascades, pools and a fine waterfall. It is quite different to the usual Lakeland gills, for the granite rock is more massive with few holds. The ravine is square-cut, with vertical walls and a very bouldery bed. The atmosphere is verdant and oppressive between the dark beetling walls. Save it for a lazy, hot summer day in a dry spell.

Approach: Park by Netherbeck Bridge on the side of Wastwater. Walk up a few hundred yards to join the main path, but soon leave it to enter the first gorge.

Route

The Lower Gorge

Height gain 50m. Walk to the first fall, defended by a deep pool. Wade the left side to gain a central rib. The next cascades are climbed by the left wall, starting with an awkward traverse on slippery rocks over a deep pool to reach a central spur. It is easier for a while, but leaps across mid-stream boulders maintain the interest. The ravine narrows, with steep walls and another wade at the right of a pool. Round a bend the final waterfall comes into view, the crux of the first gorge, where a rope may be useful. Gain the left side (possible escape here), then traverse a mossy gangway steepening into an overflow channel. The vertical lip is crossed in an exposed position, with a useful foothold on its edge.

Walk ½ mile to the second gorge which is not as beautiful as the first, but perhaps more difficult in its central part.

The Upper Gorge

Height gain 40m. Enter by a sheepfold, then there is bouldery walking to where the ravine narrows between vertical walls. There is a thigh-deep wade in dry conditions, then boulder-bed scrambling along the ravine floor. The walls heighten and overhang – slimy pink-tinged rock decked with trees and ferns. Keep right past a small cascade to a deeper pool. This is the crux. Edge thigh-deep around the left wall, then with the aid of underwater footholds gain a shelf just on the left of a small fall. Don't fall in! Pass the pool above and climb a steep step. A tangle of fallen trees often adorns the next cascade. Climb the rocks on its right. Cross another deep pool on the left then wade into the centre on a submerged rock and right of a large boulder. (There is an escape left above

In the upper gorge there are deep pools which cannot be avoided and thigh-deep wades are necessary at times. Escape is feasible in few places. The scrambling is generally easy, with just an occasional difficulty.

this.) Pass a mid-stream boulder which sprouts trees from its top, then wade a deep pool and climb the right side of huge boulders. Cross the boulders at the top to the left side along a gangway. Cross right above and complete the gorge by easier scrambling.

6. Bell Rib, Yewbarrow

Grade 3 ✳ *NY170075*

The shapely cone of Yewbarrow is very prominent on the journey up Wasdale. It is a steep-sided wedge-shaped fell with ridges at either end.

Bell Rib, Yewbarrow

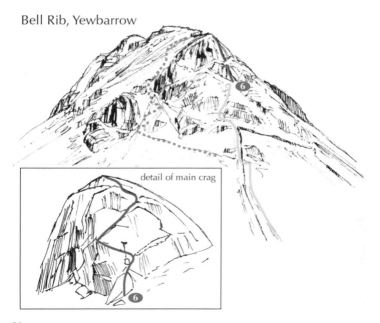

detail of main crag

Approach: There is a car park at Overbeck Bridge, directly below the steep prow of Yewbarrow. A path rises on the right of the stream then mounts the crest of the spur on the right of the wall to a stile. Over this, leave the main path and keep straight on by the wall to its top corner. Bear left and climb a steep grassy gully. At its head there is a spiky rib on the right where the scramble begins.

Route: Start on the left side of the rib and scramble up, bearing right to a grass terrace below the imposing steep buttress of Bell Rib (**best done roped**). The scramble takes

The direct way up the ridge of Yewbarrow has a short difficult section. Height gain 80m.

Difficult scrambling on Bell Rib

53

the slabby rocks right of the nose. Start at the foot of the slabs and climb to a ledge with a block, well suited for a tape runner. Move onto a heathery ramp then immediately traverse left on good footholds to a ledge on the rib. Easier-angled rock back right brings a choice of ways to zigzag to the top.

Continue along the fell top to the distinctive gap of Great Door. A descent path drops to the left, or the fell-top path goes over the summit and drops down a craggy descent to Dore Head. On the way back down the valley you could visit the **Bowderdale Boulder** GR NY166077. This is situated by the stream below Dropping Crag and provides a variety of problems pioneered in the early days of climbing at Wasdale Head.

MOSEDALE

The following three scrambles are in the deep side-valley of Mosedale, which is accessed from the Wasdale Head Inn.

7. Red Pike from Black Beck
Grade 2 ✱✱ *NY175102*

A vertical height of 540m makes this one of the longest mountaineering scrambles in the Lake District. Red Pike's Mosedale flank is very craggy and complex. This route, based on Black Beck, explores two craggy combes and ends within a few feet of the summit. In Haskett-Smith's early guide *Climbing in the British Isles* (1894), the rocks of Red Pike are mentioned. It seems as though few people have explored them since, for the combes are trackless and lonely. A chain of small craglets is linked to make a long mountaineering scramble with a little walking between sections. The whole mountainside is a

Red Pike from Black Beck

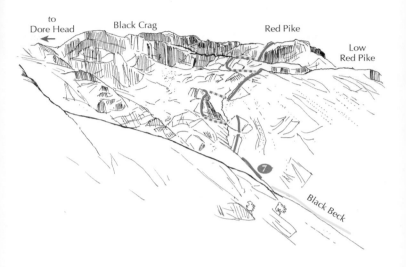

welter of crags of varying degrees of steepness, which offer scope for much variation. The route described aims to link the cleanest rocks.

Approach: Park at the green triangle at Wasdale Head. Behind the hotel cross the river at a packhorse bridge and follow a path into the flat valley of Mosedale. Pass the worn out scree shoot of Dore Head. Black Beck is the first stream which drains from Red Pike.

Route: The beck becomes interesting where it enters a narrowing past a tree. Take the right fork into a defile where the stream falls over the right wall. Climb the steep wall just left of the stream on good holds to a mossy exit. (The left branch of the stream bypasses this difficult pitch.) Black Beck issues between crags above, with the cleanest rocks to its right. (Other possible good scrambling lies on

In the beck the rock is slaty and a little of the crag scrambling is vegetated, but on the whole the rock is rough and sound – a joy to climb. Difficulties are easily avoided and there is scope for more difficult rock climbing. Avoid in damp conditions when the rock becomes treacherous.

The long scramble on Red Pike links attractive outcrops

crags well left.) Climb the rib, starting a few feet up on the left. Flake-holds lead to a grass ledge with another length of slabby rib above. This is most easily started 4m up on the right in a corner – step onto the rib and ascend it airily. After a grass ledge the rib continues. Move into a groove on the left to finish. Go up rough slabs on the left to exit on grass slopes.

The next good buttress on this side of the stream lies well above, but the crags on the left of the stream, whilst more mossy and vegetated, offer some interest to gain height. Cross the stream and walk to the left-hand end of the lower crag. Move strenuously right onto a large pointed block. Step left from its top and mount slabs. Climb a spiky ridge at the right edge of the next craglet to a mid-point ledge. The rib steepens above but can be flanked by walking right along the ledge, which turns into an exposed slab. Step round a corner – take care, as some of the foot level blocks are loose – to easy ground. Interest can be maintained by a devious traverse back above the slab onto the front of the buttress.

From the top of the knoll, walk across the stream to the foot of a clean crag of very rough rock on the right.

Start up the left end and climb steeply to a grass ledge. From the right end of this climb a steep wall onto rough slabs. A little outcrop on the right gains height to the next long stretch of slabby ribs. More slabs follow to a grass hollow where the best rocks lie well to the left. Walk along a flat shelf for about 200m. Do not go too far where the crags are steep, but aim for a narrow rib of slabs which start above a lower broken tier above the shelf. The lower tier is climbed by steep little walls, then move left to the clean sweep of slabs which emerge on the edge of the summit combe.

Crags ring the combe and it is difficult to choose the best way, for there is a lot of steep rock and much scrappy rock, with no obvious good scrambling route. However, the following proves better than it looks. Directly ahead is a steep crag reached by walking along a marshy shelf. Below the main crags are subsidiary rocks on the left of scree. Start up the rib then move right to a slab, climbed by a grassy groove on its right. The rock fizzles out into the scree below the main crag. Go directly ahead to a shallow mossy gully. Start up the gully for 6m then move onto knobbly rocks on the right. Where these run into scrappy ground, move right onto exposed slabs with good holds onto the final slopes. Walk right to a small rock block which ends a few feet from the ridge. The summit lies just to the right.

Once on the ridge there are several options. Scoat Fell and Pillar lie close by and a fine round can be made to Black Sail Pass. If you choose to descend from Red Pike by the regular route to Dore Head, be warned – the steep screes into Mosedale used to be a fine run but wore out many years ago. Now it is a dangerous bare slope with a very steep path at its side. A more interesting and very easy descent which explores the northerly craggy combe of Red Pike is as follows. Walk the ridge to the col between Red Pike and Scoat Fell. Turn right down a steep slope then bear left across a shoulder. Keeping diagonally left descend between a band of crags to a broad grassy shelf above the slabs of

Elliptical Crag. Drop down the far side of these on grass to easy grass slopes in the Mosedale valley bottom. This route completes a fine mountain day, but care must be taken to spy out the correct line from the ridge, as descent too early could be dangerous.

8. Red Pike by the Gully Slabs

Grade 2 or 3 NY166109

Worth doing for the rock crest near the top, but the rest is very mediocre. 250m height gain.

This scramble lies up the rocks well to the right of the summit. Fairly low down is a steep rock wall with a narrow buttress on its right. To the right of this is an easy-angled gully slanting up to the right, with rock slabs on its wall.

Approach: From behind the Wasdale Head Inn, cross the packhorse bridge and follow a path into Mosedale. Above the flat area follow the stream and branch left to the foot of a steep rock wall with the gully an obvious feature.

Red Pike, Gully Slabs

Red Pike

grade 3
start

Route: A grade 3 start can be made up slabs 20m right of the gully. A grassy trough running left towards the gully becomes difficult after 6m, so cross diagonally right and up to reach a thin grass ledge which leads into the gully. Otherwise avoid by walking up the gully. Keep close to the slabby edge for maximum exposure. There is a short steeper section, then easy slabs to broken ground. Walk up to where the gully bends left. Take rocks on the right in short steep steps, with a choice of keeping to the rock or avoiding it by grassy troughs. Eventually a sheep track leads left to a shelf below a sharp rock ridge. There is a delicate step on the ridge at 9m, avoided by circling left. Above, the scramble leads to the plateau.

9. Wistow Crags, Pillar

Grade 2 or 3 ✱✱✱ *NY175112*

A popular scramble, well worthwhile either as a way to the high fell tops or as a prelude to Pillar Rock. Towards the head of Mosedale there is a two-tier crag between gullies, well to the right of the worn-out scree shoot-path to Wind Gap. The route was used as an approach to Pillar Rock by the pioneers of Lakeland rock climbing, then largely forgotten until this book first appeared in 1982.

Approach: From Wasdale Head Inn, cross the packhorse bridge and follow the path into Mosedale. Another path joins from the other side of the valley. Climb the Wind Gap path for a short way then go diagonally right to the base of the crags, with gullies on either side.

Route: Start at a grass platform at the foot of the buttress. An easy initial stretch is followed by a steep wall which proves to be the crux (grade 3), but this can be avoided by a detour into the gully on the left. The wall can be climbed either by a slab on its left edge with a steep awk-ward start and widely spaced holds or, better, by a steep

Clean, rough, south-facing scrambling on the exposed crest of the buttress. Chief difficulties low down can be avoided, and the upper section varied at will. Take care with loose rock near the top. Height gain 270m. **Rope advised** for the first steep part.

Wistow Crags, Pillar

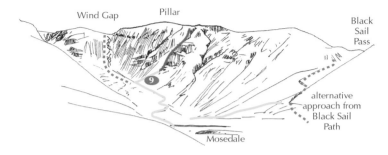

Wind Gap   Pillar   Black Sail Pass

9

alternative approach from Black Sail Path

Mosedale

Steep scrambling low down on Wistow Crags.
Photo: G.Dewitt

heathery crack on its right with an airy move right after 6m. Either way leads to the base of a fine rib to the right of the gully. Climb the rib, delicate at first, which is a fine stretch of interesting rock. An easier alternative to the start of the rib is to climb the large block on the left of the gully, which leads to nice slabs. An easier-angled broken section ends the first tier. Walk to the second tier and scramble up a broad rib to the left of a slab, or make a more difficult direct route up the slab. Walk along the ledge above to the edge of the buttress and take slabs above. The angle relents, and walking interspersed with scrambling crosses the neck at the head of the bounding gullies. Go slightly left to the rocks above. A very thin flake is best bypassed on scrappy rock to better ribs above. At the next bouldery ribs take the right hand, as the boulders on the left seem unstable. The summit ridge path is not far away.

Left along the path takes you to Pillar summit, where a cairn on the north edge of the plateau marks the path descent to Pillar Rock. This path traverses at first then drops steeply to the neck by Pisgah and High Man. Slab and Notch scramble (Route 25) is well seen from this path.

10. Ill Gill, Kirkfell

Grade 3 **✳✳✳** *NY201098*

The otherwise dull slopes of Kirkfell, facing Wasdale, contain one of Lakeland's best gill expeditions. Ill Gill is a long straight ravine on the smooth slopes facing Gavel Neese, the shoulder of Great Gable. Even from close by it is easy to walk past without noticing the steep-walled narrow ravine. The bed is composed of solid rock, there are innumerable small cascades to surmount and the trip

Despite an impassable fall which bars a complete ascent, the bulk of the scrambling is excellent. There are long stretches where escape would be difficult. **Rope advised** for the hard bits, which do involve rock climbing. Height gain 360m.

is of great beauty, best climbed in a long dry spell. There is a serious ascent of a crumbly pitch to bypass one of the falls, but this could itself be bypassed by leaving the gill altogether. For competent rock climbers a direct ascent in drought of the three main falls would present a difficult challenge.

Approach: Park at the triangle of the Green at Wasdale Head and take the rough lane ahead past the church. Go through Burnthwaite to join the path from the inn. Continue to the footbridge over Gable Beck, climb the Gavel Neese path a short way to enter the gill at its junction with Gable Beck.

The smooth water-worn trench in Ill Gill

Route: Immediately the charm of the gill is apparent, with interesting scrambling past green pools. The first obstacle is an 8m fall climbed on good holds on the steep right wall. A tiny cascade proves awkward to surmount. Just above this is a gardened escape route out of the ravine on the right wall. It is advisable to use this escape, for ahead is a difficult double cascade. (You can scramble up for a close look, bypassing the first cascade by a way up the steep grass and trees of the right wall to a basin below the main fall, which is a formidable problem. Do not be tempted to escape up the right wall for this is dangerously friable and steeper than it looks. Instead retreat to the escape.)

Walk up steep slopes bordering the ravine to just above the waterfall, where a rock rib is crossed. A scree shoot takes you easily back to the stream, but take care near the bottom not to shoot over a small drop. Start scrambling again up a succession of small cascades. One flows down a slab which is climbed just left of the watercourse on excellent holds. Above is a steep little stepped fall. Start on the right (very awkward for 3m), where you can climb up a few feet then move left round a steep rib to the easier watercourse. The next fall is more formidable, a steep wall which perhaps may be climbable in bone-dry conditions. However, there is a gardened bypass on the crumbly left wall. It requires care, for almost all the holds can be crumbled away! Now you are in a basin, with a steep recess down which the water shoots into a pool. Escape from the amphitheatre on the far right with a short ascent of steep heather. Back in the gill the sport goes on. A rising staircase leads pleasantly to a junction where a scree gully enters from the right. Follow the main rock bed, up an awkward little cascade to screes which cover the gill bed for a while. Scrambling soon returns with a pleasant little ascent of a pink-veined cascade. Finally, at a point where the main stream enters the ravine over the steep left wall, take the rocks on the left. A clean rib on the left of the stream can be ascended for a while, and it is probably best to stick to this if you are heading for Kirkfell Tarn on the summit plateau, still a rough walk away.

If you go over the north-east summit there is more scrambling on Boat Howe Crags (Routes 29, 30). The most pleasant descent to Wasdale is from the south-west summit and the path north-west to Black Sail Pass and Mosedale. If you do not want to continue to the fell top when the gill scramble fizzles out, a gruelling descent is reached by working rightwards across a steep rocky slope to reach the open hillside, where a fine scree run gives a descent, followed by steep grass to the start of the gill.

GREAT GABLE – THE NAPES

The attractive cone of Great Gable dominates the head of Wasdale, and on its sunny slopes, high amongst colourful screes, is a cluster of converging rock ridges. These are the crags of the Napes, which include the obelisk of Napes Needle, first climbed solo in 1886 by Haskett-Smith, which is perhaps the symbol of rock climbing in the Lake District. The crags are today slightly old fashioned, for most of the climbs are easy by modern standards of rock climbing, but on a good day you will generally see some teams enjoying the alpine-style rock ridges. The scrambler can visit these crags and thoroughly appreciate the impressive rock scenery without recourse to rock climbing, but care is required. There is quite a lot of loose rock about, especially off the well-trodden routes, and wherever you get a lot of people you need to be aware of the dangers from dislodged stones. For that reason it is not advisable to scramble up Needle Gully immediately above a place where people congregate at the foot of Napes Needle. **The use of helmets is wise.**

The Napes, Great Gable

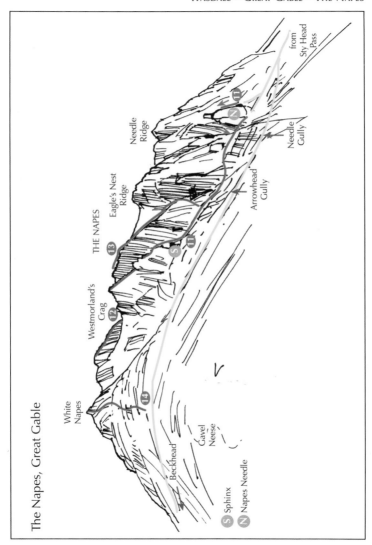

White Napes

Westmorland's Crag

THE NAPES

Eagle's Nest Ridge

Needle Ridge

from Sty Head Pass

Needle Gully

Arrowhead Gully

Beckhead

Gavel Neese

S Sphinx
N Napes Needle

11. The Napes by the Climbers' Traverse and Sphinx Ridge

*Grade 1 or 2*** NY209100*

Varied scrambling in interesting situations. Take care on the traverse to avoid any stones dislodged by climbers above. Height gain 140m.

This route combines an old favourite with some less obvious scrambling to make a route of considerable length on good clean rock. It encompasses some of the finest scenery in the Lakes as it winds its way below the rock ridges of the Napes. The grade can be varied to suit. A finish up the Pinnacle Ridge of Westmorland's Crag (Route 12) ends close to the mountain summit.

Approach: From Wasdale Head parking at the triangle of The Green, follow the rough lane past the church and Burnthwaite to join a path from the inn. This rises across the steep screes of Great Gable towards Sty Head. At a shoulder with a cairn, below the steep crag of Kern Knotts, you can take a short-cut left under the more broken Lower Kern Knotts to join the traversing path which comes from Sty Head, under Kern Knotts and continues towards the Napes. The path crosses steep screes and goes under the steep crag of Tophet Wall. Continue until the Needle comes into view. On a slight rise a lesser path rises right and into Needle Gully.

From Seathwaite at the head of Borrowdale, reach Sty Head, where a path goes right up Gable Breast to the summit. The traverse path to Kern Knotts goes left near the start of this, indistinct at first, then more defined as Kern Knotts come into view. Cross the chaotic boulders below the crags and continue more easily to the Napes. Both approaches take over 2 hours.

Route
Threading the Needle (grade 2)
A crossing of the gap between The Needle and Needle Ridge makes an interesting but difficult start. Scramble from the path to gain the base of the cleft below the right-

hand side of Napes Needle. A steep strenuous struggle ensues up the chimney to reach the narrow gap. The descent of the other side is less awkward, but is steep and highly polished by the passage of countless feet. **Rope may be useful** because of this.

Napes Needle makes an impressive backdrop to the Climbers' Traverse

The Climbers' Traverse (grade 1)

This starts opposite the base of the Needle, and is approached by a scramble up the bed of Needle Gully. Climb out of the gully on polished holds to a ledge on the left, the Dress Circle, which affords a fine vantage point of performers on the Needle. A rock path is now traversed below Eagle's Nest Ridge and across a slab. Scramble down into a gully then up again to pass through a gap behind a flake. Cross a steep little wall to descend into another gully, then continue the traverse towards the aptly named Sphinx Rock, which gazes inscrutably over the patchwork of fields in Wasdale Head far below. Just before the Sphinx reach a gully, which is followed for a short way until it is feasible to leave its unpleasant confines for the cleaner, open rocks of Sphinx Ridge.

Sphinx Ridge (grade 2)

This is reached above the steep initial buttress behind the Sphinx, in the midst of several bouldery towers. It narrows to an exposed step across a gap onto a steeper ridge. Follow this for 10m to a platform below an obviously fiercer bit of ridge, which can be avoided by a traverse of a narrow heathery ledge back into the gully. (The gully can be followed throughout, but is hardly scrambling). Gain the easier ridge and follow it for about 100m. There is a path which winds about, but it is more interesting to take all the steps direct, one being a good steep wall. There is a fine view of the other Napes Ridges, which converge into a narrow crest which is almost alpine in character, apart from the lack of snow. All the ridges meet at a sharp grassy neck.

An unpleasant stony descent can be made from here down the scree gully on the far side of the neck, through a narrows, to the path below Tophet Wall. Useful if you want to do another scramble.

The best continuation is to the mountain summit by way of the following route.

12. Pinnacle Ridge, Westmorland's Crag

Grade 2✳✳ NY209101

Approach: From the top of the Napes, instead of taking the walkers' path which bends under the crags on the left, take a slight horizontal path across red scree to the base of the rocks. Continue under one small spur to another, marked by a square-topped block at its base.

This scramble is much easier than it looks and quite entertaining. Height gain 50m.

Route: Scramble up the rocky ridge, keeping right at towers, up a series of steps. Do not escape into the gully on the right, but move left across a steep wall to reach the crest on the left. This leads to a gap at the back of a pinnacle. Once again, do not escape into the gully as this only leads to uninteresting terrain. Climb a short wall to reach the crest again, whence airy rocks lead easily to the top.

Pinnacle Ridge, Westmorland's Crag

path to summit

top of Napes Ridges

13. Eagle's Nest Gully and Arrowhead Ridge

Grade 2✱✱✱ NY208100

The gully is more difficult than Route 11 and requires care with loose stones; do not dislodge any onto people below. The ridge is airy and scenic. Height gain 140m.

Combined with Route 11 this makes just as good a day on the Napes, but is a little more difficult. This scramble follows the gully between Eagle's Nest and Arrowhead Ridge, with fine rock scenery, to culminate up the final part of Arrowhead Ridge, above the rock climbing difficulties.

Approach: Follow Route 11 along the Climbers' Traverse, from the Dress Circle, through the gap behind the large flake and into Eagle's Nest Gully. Arrowhead Ridge is on the left, the Arrowhead being a distinctive block at the top of the steep initial buttress. See diagram p.65.

Route: Scramble up rocks on the left of the gully. There is a slight track to the foot of steeper rocks, where a slanting groove cuts from left to right towards the gully above a chockstone. Follow this into the gully, then go up, avoiding a steep step by a detour on the left. Regain the main scree gully and continue to where it splits. Take the cleaner central branch and bear left towards the top to a grass shelf on the crest of the ridge. You are now above the climbing part of Arrowhead Ridge which can be seen as a sharp rock crest. The ridge continues as a rock spur with a cracked front. Climb this (awkward at first) and some boulders on the rib above which require care. From a flat rock shelf, climb slabs and the broken ridge to a grass neck. The rock scramble can be prolonged up the next rib and ends at the grassy neck at the top of the Napes to join Route 12 for the ascent of the Pinnacle Ridge of Westmorland's Crag to Great Gable summit.

There are several options for the return to Wasdale: by the Breast path to Sty Head; by the Windy Gap path into Stony Cove below Gable Crag, where a traversing path leads to Beck Head; or descend directly to Beck Head. A traverse over Kirk Fell to Black Sail Pass makes a good finish to the day.

14. The White Napes

Grade 1 NY207101

This group of rocks crowns Gavel Neese, and from below appears as an impressive rock pyramid. The route has no particular merit except the fine views of the Napes, but even these are better appreciated from closer quarters.

The rock requires care with loose blocks. Height gain 180m.

Approach: The path up the prominent spur of Gavel Neese, from the footbridge over Gable Beck, rises to the foot of the rocks where a horizontal track from Beck Head to the Napes is crossed. It must be assumed that the many walkers who continue up the scrambly rocks do not notice this track or, having become used to a steady upwards slog, do not wish to deviate. See diagram p.65.

Route: The broad buttress can be scrambled anywhere, but the rocks of the final pyramid are more continuous, especially on the right where they form an arête. The arête is too steep to climb direct, so after a start up the crest, turn onto the left flank and continue by slabs and grooves until the arête can be regained above its steepest section. The angle then relents to a horizontal crest.

THE SCAFELL RANGE

Scafell Pike is the highest point in England, but it is merely the highest summit of a broad high-level fell stretching from Great End, past Broad Crag and Ill Crag to the Pike, then dropping to the knife-edge col of Mickledore before rising in a steep crag to the less accessible summit of Scafell. Lingmell forms a lower rocky shoulder of Scafell Pike, and between Lingmell and Sty Head, the pass which connects Wasdale with Borrowdale, the mountain side is deeply riven by several important gills.

The Scafell range is complicated and interesting with a great deal of bare rock, in fact much of the fell top is composed almost entirely of rock, a rough boulder plateau where mosses and lichens predominate. However, the amount of worthwhile scrambling is limited on the Wasdale flank, for the lower crags are steep and vegetated whilst much of the higher buttresses are either not the right rock construction for scrambling or are too broken to provide more than rough walking.

Scafell itself has a majestic display of crags, but in the main these are the domain of rock climbers, although a terrace, The Rakes Progress, which undulates below the main cliff from the foot of Lord's Rake to the col of Mickledore, provides some easy scrambling at the top end. This terrace runs below a popular climbing crag and may be dangerous to unhelmeted scramblers. Pikes Crag, which faces Scafell Crag across Hollow Stones, has a sunnier aspect but again it is too steep to be of much interest to the scrambler and its gullies are unattractive. Lingmell, a lower rocky shoulder, has impressive crags which drop into the ravine of Piers Gill, but they are vegetated and shattered.

Piers Gill is the most obvious feature of the lower mountainside. It is a striking ravine which looks as though it has been wrenched apart. To its north a succession of smaller ravines follow the same pattern and were probably produced by the same forces to create deep ravines with shattered vegetated walls and impressive

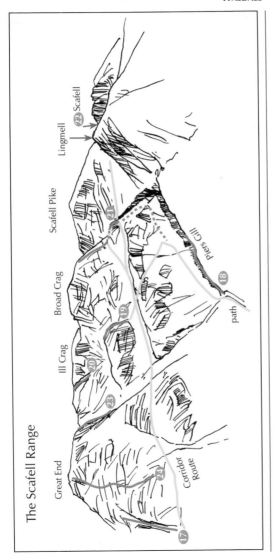

The Scafell Range

waterfalls. A natural shelf, above the steep crags and ravines, is used by the Corridor Route, a popular walkers' path from Sty Head to the Pike. Above this path, in the combe between Great End and Broad Crag, is the glaciated rock knoll of Round How, with a craggy combe behind. The range culminates in the steep crags of Great End, overlooking Grains Gill and Borrowdale.

THE WASDALE RAVINES

From Great End to Lingmell the Wasdale side of the mountain is riven by several fault-controlled ravines. The largest and most renowned is **Piers Gill**, a magnificent but severe rock-climbing scramble feasible only in drought. The left-hand offshoot of Piers Gill is **Greta Gill**, narrow and straight, with nothing for the scrambler as impassable waterfalls bar the way. Left again are two small ravines past Stand Crag – **Grainy Gills**, the right fork, does offer some scrambling in its lower part. The final fault lies in the valley stream itself, **Spout Head Gill**, which is worth incorporating into the day's sport.

15. Spout Head Gill

Grade 2 or 3✳ NY214091

Good quality rock and interesting stream scenery make this short scramble worthwhile. Height gain 90m.

Approach: Park at the Wasdale Head Green and follow the track along the valley to where the main Sty Head path starts to rise, not far past the Gable Beck footbridge. Fork right on the old pony track, cross the stream and pass the confluence of Piers Gill to the next confluence, where Spouthead Gill is the main valley stream.

Route: The first real obstacle is a 10m cascade climbed by a steep spiky rib on the left. A gentle rock bed leads to more risers. The first, by a tree, follows a bypass; the second takes a central rib to finish up the trough of the

Spout Head Gill

stream. Past a pool enter a deeper ravine, where a cascade presents a more formidable obstacle by the rocks on its left wall (grade 3). Alternatively retreat and climb the left edge of the ravine entrance (grade 2). Mount easy risers to a slabby cascade which makes an excellent pitch. Start on the left up a steep damp wall. Cross the spray to the right side of the cascade and finish up its narrow trough. Climb a broad barrier at its right. The fault ends where the stream cascades over its steep left wall – make a way up this.

On the right is the old pony track which makes a useful descent to the foot of Grainy Gill (Route 16). Alternatively, continue up the pony track to reach the Corridor path to access the scramble on Round How (Route 19).

16. Grainy Gill
Grade 2 NY215091 🌿🌿

A short scramble, more mossy and grassy than the preceding, but there are some good pitches and impressive situations, although the route is feasible only half-way up the ravine. Height gain 120m.

Approach: Best done after Spouthead Gill (Route 15) – this is the right-hand stream at the confluence. Two parallel streams run in faults up the hillside; the right-hand one is larger and carries more water.

Route: At first there is easy open scrambling in a succession of small risers above deep little pools. A 10m waterfall bars access to the main ravine. Climb a rib on the left to regain slabs above the fall. Climb to another deep cleft capped by a chockstone. A direct ascent seems improbable, and retreat from below the chock is awkward on splintered rock. Avoid it and regain the stream at a bend above. The small fall above is sporting with good holds at the top. The deep ravine above is ascended to a spectacular jammed block. Pass this on the left to a ledge then surmount a bulge onto the top of the block. This may require a helping push. Progress above is barred by a series of impressive falls.

Fortunately there is a steep escape possible on the right wall, and the route is best ended here.

A steep walk joins the Corridor path.

17. Skew Gill
Grade 1 NY221091 🔺 🥾

The last of the ravines between Piers Gill and Great End is a tapering scree gully. See diagrams p.73 and for Route 24.

Approach: The pony track on the right of Spouthead Gill leads directly to the scree gully, crossing the Corridor path at its base.

Route: The narrowing scree gully poses no route-finding problems. At its top bear left to join the path to Great End summit.

The following three routes make a logical scramble onto the fell top, but are advisable only in dry conditions.

The gully is well used as a way up Great End, but the rocks are loose and require care. 150m height gain.

18. Piers Gill (first part only)
Grade 1✳ NY214086 🔺 🥾

Of necessity, this has to be a brief foray, as a complete ascent involves some severe rock climbing and requires drought conditions! However, the ravine can be penetrated quite easily to the first waterfalls. This route provides an impressive short visit into the most dramatic of Lakeland's gills. See diagram p.73.

Approach: From the parking at Wasdale Head Green, follow the valley track towards Sty Head. Shortly after the

Very deep shattered side-walls and views of the crags of Lingmell give some indication of the seriousness of a complete ascent. Height gain 70m.

footbridge over Gable Beck fork right on the old pony track and cross the stream just past the confluence with Lingmell Beck. Leave the pony track for a tiny path above the left edge to the confluence of Greta Gill and Piers Gill.

Route: The ravine begins as a clamber over a bouldery bed then becomes more scrambly just before a small side-stream enters on the left. The walls are now much closer and the first real problems are encountered at two thin cascades. The first can be traversed awkwardly on the left wall, but remember you have to retreat the same way! This is as far as this route goes; to ascend further includes at least three serious pitches, a passage of the Bridge Rock, and few chances of escape.

Scramblers can only explore the first part of Piers Gill before it becomes too difficult

After your look into Piers Gill you need to reach Round How for the next scramble. There are steep crags above, but the following way avoids them and emerges on the shelf at the Corridor Route at exactly the right place. There is a path on the left edge of Piers Gill. Follow this past a deep-cut little side-stream towards a band of crag above. Before reaching this crag, branch left across grass slopes, seek a suitable place to recross the deep-cut little ravine, then continue in the same rising leftwards line to a grass col above the lower crags. Round How soon comes into view directly opposite. An easier continuation is on Broad Crag (Route 21) a little further right.

19. Round How

Grade 3✱✱ NY217081

Round How

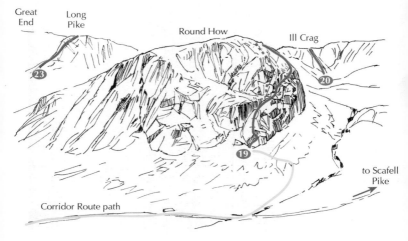

Great End

Long Pike

Round How

Ill Crag

23

20

19

to Scafell Pike

Corridor Route path

Some route-finding ability is required to keep to the easy line, and the upper part is somewhat exposed. **A rope is comforting in places.** Height gain 90m.

A rocky glaciated knoll above the track of the Corridor Route and below Broad Crag is bigger than it looks and provides an excellent scramble, in dry conditions. Slabs, corners and shelves of rough-textured rock combine to make an intricate route with two difficult passages. The first is low down on the slabs; the second just above the easy escape terrace.

Approach: The most interesting approach is by Route 18. Alternatively, follow the Corridor Route from Sty Head which traverses the mountainside below Skew Gill, crosses Greta Gill and gains the grassy shelf below Round How. The route takes the slabs at the far right end.

Route: The south-west corner of Round How contains attractive slabs. Start at the foot of these. A ledge runs up, right, to a groove. The exit from this is up a short corner (good small nut runner) surmounted by a knee in the groove and a long reach to a good hold. Now climb easy-angled rough rocks on the nose just left of a little

Scrambling on the lower slabs of Round How

groove. At its top move right to more rough rocks to a grass terrace, with a small flake belay. Escape is possible here. The route continues in the same line, rising slabs trending right. Just above the terrace is a slabby corner groove (for a variant to the groove, see below) which is awkward for a few feet especially if damp, but the angle is easy and small holds appear. Cross a wide juniper terrace to its right end and go up ledges on the right, past the lower of two perched blocks. Climb up to a ramp which rises to the right, over a block. Continue at that level then up to a juniper ledge. Mossy mantelshelves left of an overhanging nose lead easily to a large grassy bay with boulders. Step from the large boulder onto a fine sweep of slabs on the right. Go up the front of these, moving left into a groove near the top to reach a terrace. Gain a rock ledge on the slab above to the left and go up a groove. A series of steps is scrambled to the top, which provides a good viewpoint.

Variant

A well-used alternative, if the groove is too wet, is by the clean rib on its left. Climb a groove on good holds to a steepening with an awkward exit onto a rounded ledge. Follow the easiest way up corners, grooves and slabs to the top.

Behind Round How is a marshy hollow backed by a rocky combe between Great End and Broad Crag. On the left is the impressive buttress of Long Pike (Route 23); on the right the steep broken rocks of Broad Crag (Route 21). Between them, at the back of the combe, just left of the highest point, is a sweep of clean slabs (Route 20), just left of a slanting scree gully. These catch the afternoon sun and make a fine continuation to Route 19 and a satisfying way of reaching the fell-top plateau.

20. North-West Combe, Ill Crag

Grade 2✱ NY223078

Rough-textured
rocks, just steep
enough to make an
interesting route.
Height gain 70m.

Approach: From Round How, cross the boggy bottom and follow a small stream into the combe and along by the side of scree to the foot of the slabs, the lowest rocks on the left of the slanting gully. See diagram p.73 and for Route 19.

Route: Climb a blunt arête to a grass ledge below a steepening. Take a left-slanting mossy groove to a grass ledge. Continue in the same line by a stepped gangway up left, then back right to a terrace about 12m right of the arête. Climb a steep clean nose above on good holds just left of a mossy break. This leads to a sweep of clean slabs to make a good finish.

The following is an easier alternative to the Round How scramble, and a good way of using rock to reach the summit plateau.

21. South-West Buttress, Broad Crag

Grade 1 NY216077

Easy but pleasant
scrambling if the
rock is sought; it
makes a more
interesting alterna-
tive to the path.
Height gain 200m.

The right-hand side of the broken crags of Broad Crag is rough, solid and easy angled. One can scramble anywhere, but the described line takes the most continuous rocks. See diagram p.73.

Approach: The scramble can be started where the Corridor Route path crosses the top of Piers Gill, or from a higher-level path which slants from the foot of Round How to below the main crags at a cairn. (The path continues into a scree combe to the right of the crags and up to the col between Broad Crag and Scafell Pike.)

Route: Above the Corridor Route at the top of Piers Gill is a short rock buttress. Climb this by steep little walls to a rocky, almost horizontal crest. Walk along this to the upper path at the cairn on a small col. The best rock buttress is directly above. Go up the rocks slightly right towards the edge of the buttress. From a grass terrace on the right a fine sweep of rock leads up, at first by easy scrambling over ledges to a grass terrace below an obviously more difficult wall. Walk left and climb a short steep 3m crack on good holds to another ledge on the left. There are no further difficulties, but plenty of rock to incorporate. Above a large grass shoulder a final sweep of slabs leads to the top.

Scafell Pike, the highest point of England, is a short stroll away, whilst Scafell, across the gap of Mickledore, is defended by the short steep scramble of Broad Stand.

22. Broad Stand, Scafell

Grade 3✳✳✳ *NY210068*

The direct ridge route between Scafell Pike and Scafell is barred by steep crags immediately past the col of Mickledore. It was first described as a descent by Samuel Coleridge in 1802, making it the first recorded scramble in the Lake District. This notorious well-polished obstacle tempts many walkers, and is a scramblers' trip into mountaineering history. It is too short to be a really good scramble, yet is a classic way to the summit of Scafell.

Approach: Mickledore is gained by a variety of paths or scrambles on Scafell Pike or directly from the NT campsite in Wasdale by the path up Brown Tongue and Hollow Stones in about 2 hours.

The crucial corner is steep, often greasy and situated above a sloping platform where a slip could be serious. Even experienced climbers **rope up for this in poor conditions**. Height gain 40m.

Broad Stand, Scafell

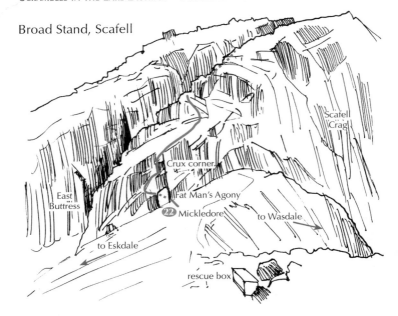

Route: Start a few metres down the Eskdale side of Mickledore at a narrow cleft (Fat Man's Agony) in the rocks on the right. Squeeze through this and circle left on shelving rock to reach a sloping platform below a steep 2.8m corner, the exposed ascent of which is the only difficulty. It is climbed by its left wall on polished holds, easiest for the tall and agile. Another shelving corner is surmounted, then easy scrambling and walking – with an excursion into the cleft of Mickledore Chimney – leads to the top of Scafell.

Descent to Wasdale is easy to the west. Alternatively Mickledore can be reached by the much improved path past Foxes Tarn and a subsequent reascent to the col. The once popular Lord's Rake is no longer advised as it is unpleasantly unstable.

*Broad Stand ascends the steep barrier to give a
direct route from Mickledore to Scafell summit*

23. Long Pike Buttress, Great End

Grade 3 ✶✶ *NY223083*

Careful route finding is needed to pick a way through steep ground, particularly in the upper part. Generally sound rock, but very slippery if damp. Some loose holds require care. **Rope advised.** Height gain 100m.

This is the narrow buttress high on the western flank of Great End. See diagrams p.73 and for Route 19.

Approach: It makes a logical continuation to the scramble on Round How (Route 19), from where it is seen across the combe to the left. A more direct approach from the Corridor Route is by the upper stream of Greta Gill. Long Pike is the obvious large broken crag with a pointed summit.

Long Pike Buttress, Great End.
Photo: G.Dewitt

Route: Follow a series of stepped edges from the foot of the crag to the lowest of a succession of smooth slabs. Ignore these, for they are smoother and steeper than they appear. Instead go leftwards until it is possible to climb a short steep wall which gives access to a long broken ridge littered with huge blocks. Go up the ridge until the angle increases and climb a series of steeper blocks and grooves until an impasse is reached. Traverse to the right, crossing a deep chimney, then rightwards again over slabs until it is possible to get up onto a broad grassy ledge. Walk right to a broken chimney and climb this to the summit of the crag.

The scramble on the slabs of Ill Crag north-west combe (Route 20) is easily reached on the right.

24. Great End from the Corridor Path

Grade 2 NY221088

The steep crags of Great End above Sprinkling Tarn are of no interest to the scrambler, but round the corner towards Wasdale the mountain presents a less steep but rocky face. The crags can be avoided easily by a zigzag walk, but if a direct ascent is taken a long scramble can be made – on rock almost all the way from the Corridor Path to the summit.

Approach: From Sty Head, as easily reached from Borrowdale as Wasdale, take the path towards Esk Hause. The Corridor Path branches right after a slight ascent, or take a less distinct short cut. Follow the Corridor Path across the crumbly foot of Skew Gill and through a natural rock gateway. About 200m past this, the path levels. The route starts just above.

Route: Start at slabs just above the right end of a long low wall of crag about 16m above the path. Cairn. Climb a

A lot of rough rock, some interesting pitches and much very easy scrambling. Marred by its north-westerly aspect which promotes green patina on the rock; thus it stays unpleasantly greasy after rain. A good mountaineering exercise with almost aerial views into Piers Gill. Height gain 250m.

Great End from the Corridor Path

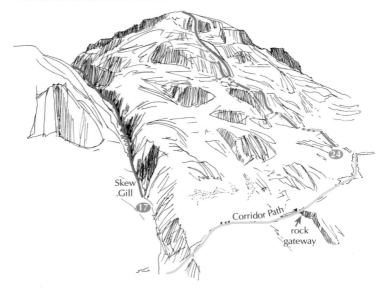

grassy groove and the rib on its right. Go left at its top to a grass terrace below a steep crag. Climb a subsidiary craglet with an overhang, by easy rocks at its right edge, to reach the foot of the steep crag. Ahead is a finger stone on the skyline. Start at the mossy groove below this and immediately move left on ledges. Climb easier-angled rock just right of the edge to finish up a recess left of the stone. Above another grassy slope are the next crags. Go diagonally up left to a knot of rock below the main crag. The front of this is climbed for 15m. Start by a ledge, right, into a small groove. Exit left and up to a bilberry ledge. Step left to gain the next ledge, with exits left. Take care at the top with its piled blocks. Directly ahead is a green slabby rib flanked by mossier rock. This would make a fine pitch if perfectly dry. An easier way is to start about

4m right, climb to the base of the rib, but escape right-wards on ledges to a recess. Edge left round the base of a block to gain a grass ledge on the slabs, with easy rocks left. Cross boulders to gain a sweep of cracked slabs, climbed at a flake on the right side, which is difficult at first. Cross a scree gully to better rock on the left.

The bands of crag go on and on, but the angle is now easier and the scrambling undistinguished, over a jumble of blocks and slabs. The rocks are smoother and it is diffi-cult to make a satisfactory route if greasy. Go left to a better rib. Reach a flat grass terrace with a short, steep crag. Climb a right-slanting groove under an overhang, or avoid it to the right. Continue easily to another terrace. Walk right 30m to the base of a short rock pyramid and climb the right edge of this. The final mossy crags lie ahead. Climb a subsidiary rib to steep rocks. Go left across a block into a short grass groove to gain the crest of a rib. Avoid the next part on grass to the right and exit with great care up a corner topped by loose scree. Climb a rib on the right to a grass platform with an overhang. Climb this on the left, sporting, by a traverse right on the lip of the overhang to climb the flake above. Swing left at top. An easier way goes straight up to this. A short boulder field leads to a small cairn on the edge of the summit plateau. The main summit lies ahead.

For a scramble on Esk Pike (Route 118, vol. 1), walk down the boulder-strewn slopes to Esk Hause, where the attractive knot of crag at the head of Eskdale is seen straight ahead.

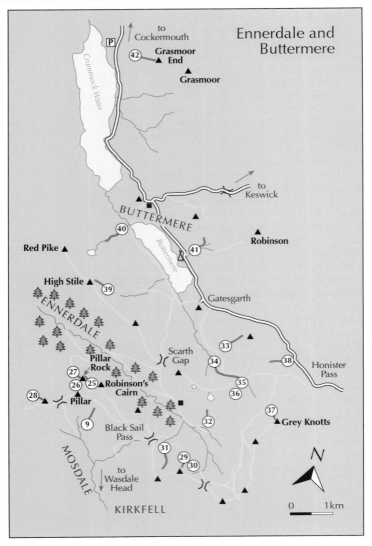

Ennerdale and Buttermere

ENNERDALE

Pillar Rock is the pride of Ennerdale and the goal of many. The Old West is a pilgrimage into the beginnings of rock climbing in Britain. Most people, apart from those living in West Cumbria, approach from the neighbouring valleys as there are vehicle restrictions in Ennerdale itself which make a long approach. Wasdale is the most favoured base, with a fine walk to Pillar Rock over Black Sail Pass and the High Level path. Buttermere provides another alternative, with Scarth Gap the access pass. Black Sail Youth Hostel at the head of Ennerdale is a fine base, but is booked up well in advance. Apart from Pillar Rock, there is some scrambling on Kirkfell. At the valley head Gable Crag, so often greasy, has been ignored for the purpose of this book. Any scrambling there is very serious, steep and grassy.

Car parking
There is a car park at Bowness Knotts; no traffic is allowed further up Ennerdale without special permission. Most scramblers will use parking at Wasdale Head or Gatesgarth in Buttermere, or at Honister Pass.

PILLAR ROCK

This is one of Lakeland's famous crags, a prized summit. The full frontal height of the crag is almost 200m. The short back is connected to the mountain by a narrow neck and the subsidiary rock hump of Pisgah. A day spent here is to savour the atmosphere of Lakeland's climbing history and marvel at the boldness of the original explorers who scrambled without the advantage of modern footwear and safety equipment.

25. Pillar Rock by Slab and Notch

Grade 3✱✱✱ NY172123

This is the popular classic way of reaching the summit of the imposing rock, first climbed in 1861. The varied ascent, which provides a lot of interest, is well trodden and very popular. However, take care, for the route is above steep crags with considerable exposure and the consequences of a slip would be grave. Allow about 3 hours from Wasdale.

Approach: The majority of first-time visitors use the High Level path which traverses the steep Ennerdale flank of the mountain. Reach the top of Black Sail Pass – most easily from Wasdale via Mosedale or (longer) from Gatesgarth in Buttermere over Scarth Gap. From the pass turn along the broad ridge towards Pillar and, where the

Pillar Rock from Robinson's Cairn

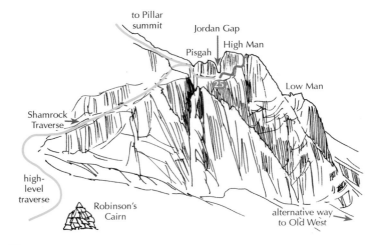

Slab and Notch, Pillar Rock

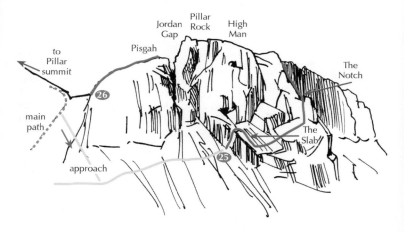

path begins to rise steeply, look for a small cairn. This marks the start of the High Level path on the right, which undulates across several steep combes. Reach Robinson's Cairn, a monument to one of the pioneers of Pillar climbing and the discoverer of the path. Here the full expanse of Pillar Rock's eastern side is seen. Your scramble is still well above, for it is only on the summit rocks. A path mounts scree to reach the Shamrock Traverse, cutting across a rising shelf above steep crags towards the neck which joins Pillar Rock to the mountain. On the left of High Man and separated from it by Jordan Gap is the lesser summit of Pisgah. The main path continues to the neck above Pisgah, but you need to gain the gully below Jordan Gap. Traverse the steep broken crags into the gully, or, nearer the rocks of Pisgah, descend a rocky cleft and a shorter traverse leads into the gully. The gently inclined slab of your route should have been identified, as it is a prominent feature just to the right of the gully.

The holds are everywhere good, but great care is required. Two short ascents are quite steep and the final gully can be greasy. **A rope for protection** is advised for all but competent rock climbers. There are good belay places. Remember also that you have to descend the same way. Height gain of 50m.

93

The Slab, on Slab and Notch

Route: From the gully, easy steps on the right wall lead up and right onto the slab. Descend this to a small horizontal ledge right into a recess below the Notch, a gap in the arête on the left of a small tower. Ascend steeply on good holds to the Notch, where a short level ledge takes you round the foot of a groove to another steep but easy ascent of an arête on excellent holds to a platform and flake belay. Move into the gully on the right, where a slabby corner is climbed to perched blocks. Move right and down into the cleft, which is scrambled to the top.

26. Pisgah
Grade 1 ✽ NY171123

This, the lesser neighbour of Pillar Rock, offers some compensation for anyone who does not wish to undertake

The lesser summit of Pisgah, in front of High Man, gives an easy scramble

the more difficult scramble onto Pillar Rock. See diagram p.93. The short ascent is made on good rock from the neck, where the main path arrives. The top is finely situated. A much more difficult (grade 3) ascent can be made directly from Jordan Gap.

After completing the ascent of Pillar Rock a steep path mounts to the fell top. A fine return to Wasdale is by way of Scoat Fell, Red Pike and Yewbarrow.

27. Pillar Rock, the Old West Route

Grade 3✱✱✱ NY172124

The Old West splits into two sections – a diagonal ascent between steep rock faces to the top of Low Man, then a steeper ascent of walls and terraces to High Man. **It is best done as a roped scramble** to ensure safety in rock-climbing situations. The first section (grade 2) is well worn, as it forms the climbers' descent from Low Man. Height gain 90m.

The original way up Pillar Rock makes a great scrambling route, particularly so since the descent is made by the Slab and Notch. Both are similar in difficulty, although the Old West has its awkward step high in an exposed position. The line of the first ascent up the final rocks of High Man is uncertain, but there is no doubting the courage and boldness of John Atkinson, an Ennerdale cooper, who made the first ascent alone in 1826.

The route is best appreciated when no one else is on the Rock, when the aura of a big mountain crag oozes from every mossy rock and overhang. I climbed here on many occasions in the 1950s when the place was swarming with climbers. Today's rock athletes prefer more easily accessible crags.

Approach: The walk to Pillar is quite long, around 3hrs – long enough to take advantage of afternoon sun on the west face. The traditional approach is by Mosedale from Wasdale Head, described in the approach to Route 25. At Robinson's Cairn the Rock comes into view. Cross a shallow combe and the path rises up a small scree. (Note the other track, which descends through a gap to the foot of the main face.) Ascend right, across the top of Shamrock, through a little gap, towards the neck at the top of High

Old West Route, Pillar Rock

High Man

Jordan Gap

Pisgah

approach gully descent

Low Man

27 alternative approach from Ennerdale

Robinson's Cairn

Low Man

27

High Man

25

Shamrock

descent gully

path to summit

Pisgah

Plan of Pillar Rock

97

From the top of Low Man, the Old West Route ascends steep walls to the summit of Pillar Rock

Man and Pisgah. Leave your sacks here (see plan). Descend the steep loose gully on the west side of Pisgah where it joins the path on the neck. It soon improves and a slight path is found out left, which zigzags into the combe below the West Face.

An **alternative approach** around the foot of Pillar Rock is longer and more arduous. A lot of height is lost to avoid the waterfall gully on the right of the Rock. Go well right up a very steep hillside to join a path from Ennerdale which slants into the combe below the West Face. This route gives splendid views of the towering rock, and one can fully appreciate the grandeur of the crag.

From Ennerdale a footbridge almost opposite the Rock gives access to a direct approach.

A **scrambling alternative approach** is from Mosedale by Wistow Crags (Route 9). Cross the top of the mountain and descend a steep path, cairn at the top, to the neck above Pillar Rock.

Route: There is an obvious diagonal line of weakness which separates the West Face from Low Man. Start at the foot of a light-coloured flare of rock in the centre of the face. This is at the foot of the popular climbs of Rib and Slab, and New West. Cross a ledge, left, into a deeper corner and go up diagonally left past the foot of another deep groove capped high up by a huge overhang. Gain a ledge and block on the rib beyond (24m). Continue along the rising ramp leftwards, cross a sloping slab (slippery if damp), and climb the right edge of a shallow gully for 8m. Cross left to a ledge and belay spike (30m). A path now leads horizontally left to easy ground on the crest. Zigzag up to a rock tooth and cairn on top of **Low Man**.

The rocks of **High Man** lie above. There is a small spike belay a few feet up the path at the foot of steep rocks. Climb up for 6m then drop left over a slab and down 6m to a grass recess – or gain this by a leftwards ascent from the start. Exit left easily onto the base of a ramp. Climb left to the foot of a grass rake. The ascent continues directly, but it may be worth going up the rake to belay. From the base of the grass rake, climb 6m to a platform, then move right on shelves for 5m. The steep ascent above is the crux of the route. Ascend to a perched block and climb the steep cracked wall above. The pull out seems suspect, but the block appears firmly wedged. Easier rocks follow to the top. Where you gain the summit, Slab and Notch lies in the deep gully on the left.

Descent: Slab and Notch *Grade 3 ✳✳✳*

Go down the narrow cleft on the east side of the summit. Where the gully widens, obvious holds cross the slab to the right (facing out) and down to reach a ledge with a huge flake block. Descend steeply on good holds to another ledge which leads, right, to the Notch. Flake belay. A steep descent on the other side of the gap is straightforward if you are tall enough. Cross to the Slab and ascend it to drop off the far side in the gully between High Man and Pisgah. Scramble left to the path and the neck between Pisgah and the mountain to complete the circuit. Alternatively, make a difficult grade 3 steep ascent of Pisgah from Jordan Gap just above, then an easy slabby scramble takes you back to your sac at the neck.

A steep path above leads to the plateau summit of Pillar, where a fine ridge walk over Scoat Fell and Red Pike is a popular return to Wasdale.

✳ ✳ ✳

28. Black Crag, West Buttress, Windgap Cove

Grade 1 or 2 NY162117

Windgap Cove lies west of Pillar, on the Ennerdale side of Scoat Fell. Mirk Cove is a shallower high-level cove to the west below the impressive little rock peak of Steeple. Black Crag crowns the head of Windgap Cove, and the large broken West Buttress lies at its right end and forms the edge of Mirk Cove.

Approach: The only merit is as a filler after scrambling elsewhere, and the best approach is from the col at the head of Mirk Cove. Descend easily to a platform at the foot of what appears to be a broken ridge on the right.

Route: From the grass platform the ridge dissolves into the right edge of a broken buttress. There is a gully with a prominent yellow jammed block near its top. Your route finds an interesting way up this. The left wall of the gully is a clean slab. Follow the rib of this to where it steepens, make a detour into the gully and return to the nice rib as soon as possible. About 12m below the yellow block, where it steepens, move left 4m onto the next easier rib. Past the block the scramble fizzles out amongst large boulders.

Clean rough rock, attractive to handle, but the crags are quite broken and a good long scramble is difficult to string together. 130m height gain.

KIRKFELL

A steep-sided mountain with a plateau top, Kirkfell suffers from the proximity of its higher neighbours, Great Gable and Pillar, yet the crags that rim the plateau and drop into the head of Ennerdale have a quiet remote charm which makes it worth a visit. The rock has a sandpaper texture, most pleasant to handle.

29. Boat Howe, East Buttress

Grade 3✳✳ NY202111

Approach: From the cols at either side of Kirkfell a linking track runs under the crags on the northern slopes. This can be reached easily from Honister Pass, via Moses' Trod, the reputed smuggler's track which contours under Green and Great Gable to Beck Head.

East Buttress, Boat Howe

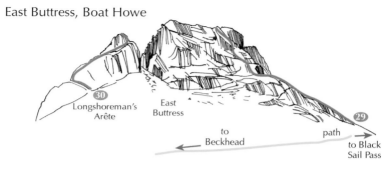

to Beckhead

path

to Black Sail Pass

At first a slabby spur, which steepens into a buttress. A long route of some character, about 160m vertical height, on excellent rock and best ascended in dry conditions. Greasy when wet.

Alternatively, gain Black Sail Pass from Wasdale or Ennerdale to pick up the linking track. Boat Howe Crags are about half-way between the two cols, and the East Buttress is the broad rambling rocky mass towards the Beck Head side of the crags.

Route: The slabby spur almost reaches the path. Start at the lowest rocks and climb a delicate slab right of the nose. Walk left to the next slabs and climb these in the centre. Above is a grooved wall, climbed from left to right, then slabs climbed on their right edge. More slabs are encountered, now with the upper buttress presenting a fine sight. The Prow of the Boat is also visible on the right, a preserve of rock climbers but rarely visited. Move left to the edge of the spur to find the most continuous rock, and reach a prominent steeper nose. There is a nice little gangway on its left, which gives an excellent pitch to a grass shelf. Climb the rocks towards a short chimney and avoid it on the left. The broadening buttress above leads to a smooth slab in a recess where the rocks steepen and the route becomes more serious. Climb the right side of the slab for a few feet to a grass ledge then mount a break on the right, followed by a rock staircase. Move right past a square block which can be used as a belay for the next crux pitch, a mossy corner groove. This is ascended on good holds to a flake belay at its top. Continue up a heathery wall and trend left to easier-angled ground where an ascending rake leads to the plateau.

A descent of Route 30 is interesting.

30. Longshoreman's Arête

Grade 1 NY203109

From below this narrow buttress, to the left of the East Buttress, presents an imposing aspect and is quite tempting for the scrambler. However, the rocks are not as long or interesting as the East Buttress, but they can be incorporated into the descent, after completing Route 29.

A narrow buttress which proves to be easy, mainly on grass amid interesting surroundings. 80m height loss.

Approach: Identification from the top is easy – NY 20241082. It presents a narrow almost horizontal crest at a slightly lower level, easily seen from the edge as one goes towards Beck Head.

Route: Walk easily along the crest to a steepening and descend heathery ledges on the left flank. A steep little rock wall is encountered just above a square-topped block. Scramble easily but carefully down past several doubtful spikes to the block. Easy walking follows to a neck and straightforward descent either side.

31. Kirkfell Gill (Sail Beck)

Grade 4✳ NY194113

This impressive ravine is well seen from the Black Sail path on its Ennerdale side. It lies on the same fault as the renowned Ill Gill on the opposite side of the mountain. It is possible to avoid the two main

A climbers' scramble of some difficulty, rarely in condition. A long period of dry weather is essential, and the ascent includes rock-climbing pitches of 'v diff' standard. 100m height gain.

pitches by coming out of the gill, but this rather spoils the expedition.

Approach: Not far below the top of Black Sail Pass on the Ennerdale side, the Kirkfell traverse path crosses the foot of the ravine.

Route: Scramble up the ravine to the first serious obstacle, a slabby cascade climbed by an ascending traverse of the left wall. A waterfall above is avoided on its left. More level scrambling in the rock bed leads to a pool backed by a cascade. Scramble to a shelf on the left then cross to the foot of the waterfall on the right. This is climbed on reasonable holds in the watercourse. Continue over a chockstone to easier scrambling to the foot of an impassable cascade. Leave the gill and re-enter above. Further difficulties are encountered before a long stretch of scrambling completes the ascent.

✳ ✳ ✳

32. Seavy Knott

Grade 3 ✳ *NY203122*

Better than it looks; definite holds and rough-textured rock, but the crag is serious and contains many loose blocks. **A rope should be used for safety**, but care should be taken to avoid flicking off stones. Height gain 80m.

An isolated scramble at the secluded head of Ennerdale, above Loft Beck. It is not worth a visit for its own sake, but is pleasantly situated with a sunny aspect and fine views. The described line purposely takes a zigzag course.

Approach: Above Black Sail Hostel, the valley floor is filled with drumlins. Seavy Knott is a crag amongst steep heather overlooking the drumlins. The Coast-to-Coast Path rises up Loft Beck immediately below. From this, slant diagonally left to the lowest outcrop with a tree.

Route: The first outcrop has a small tree. Either climb the steep difficult rib on the right or the easy slab 6m left.

Seavy Knott gives a secluded scramble at the head of Ennerdale.
Photo: G.Dewitt

Above is a steep broken wall with a tiny sapling at its foot. Go slightly right from the tree to a ledge at 6m. From the right end of this climb just left of the edge then cross, right, over heather to belay. Climb a rib above then bear left below overhangs to a good spike belay block on easy-angled rock. (This point can be gained more directly by a route from the middle of the starting ledge.) Go rightwards to a slab which leads diagonally right to a small block belay below the right edge of the bulging headwall. Climb a ramp at the base of the steep wall, moving diagonally right to a sapling. Move left onto a ledge and up the steep wall by its right edge. Move left onto the buttress front, then onto easy rocks to the top.

BUTTERMERE

The flat floor of the valley is occupied as much by water as by meadow, and the impression is of silvery lakes surrounded by steep-sided fells. On the north-eastern slopes Skiddaw Slates form smooth but shapely hills, sometimes with shattered crags unsuitable for good scrambling. More rugged are the volcanic fells which wall the valley on its west, where Red Pike, High Stile and High Crag make an attractive group. The valley head has Fleetwith Pike with the impressive Honister Crag, but heavy vegetation limits the scrambling opportunities. At the lower end of the valley the only good scrambling is on the bulky western end of Grasmoor. Buttermere is not a suitable area for novice scramblers. Apart from Grey Crag and Grey Knotts, the rock is not as friendly as in other parts of the Lake District, often lacking positive holds and being slow to dry.

There are campsites at Gatesgarth, Hassness, Buttermere and Low Lorton.

Car parking and transport

There are pay car parks at Buttermere and Gatesgarth. Parking in the rest of the valley is adequate. A Honister Rambler bus service links Keswick and Buttermere.

WARNSCALE BOTTOMS

The head of Buttermere is split by Fleetwith Pike into Gatescarthdale, which carries the Honister Pass road, and Warnscale Bottoms. The contrast is marked. Warnscale is a flat-bottomed valley head ringed by sombre black heavily vegetated crags and cut by several deep gills, unsuitable for scrambling. The area is saved by the crags on the sunny southerly flank of Fleetwith Pike. These are also heavily vegetated, but amongst the lush growth a diagonal sweep of clean rock catches the eye. This is Striddle Crag, itself part of an impressive buttress in the mountainside. Gatescarthdale has no worthwhile scrambling apart from Honister Crag at its head.

33. Striddle Crag Buttress

Grade 4✶ NY202139

A satisfying mountaineering ascent, this scramble provides an interesting way to the summit of Fleetwith Pike, although the approach is rather daunting up steep slopes of grass, scree and heather. However, the general rock scenery is ample recompense.

Approach: Park at Gatesgarth and follow a broad gentle track into Warnscale Bottoms. Take to the left hillside

Striddle Crag

Fleetwith Pike

A mixture of rock and heather scrambling, broadly based on the buttress, but with assistance from the gully on its right. The upper buttress is serious, vegetated and exposed. **A rope is strongly advised** for protection. It is possible to bypass this upper section by recourse to the gully on the right, but this detracts from the overall line. 300m height gain.

before the main screes are reached and head for the lowest part of the clean rock buttress. Keeping well to the left of the stream, a grassy rake can be followed up rightwards to the toe of the buttress.

Route: The ascending grassy rake, with a path of sorts, leads under the buttress to the edge of the gully. Progress appears hopeless, but scramble down into the square-cut recess, sprayed by water from the cascade. On the right behind a tree is a steep 3m crack, with useful tree holds. This is the key, and after a strenuous ascent the path continues, right, across a steep crag, then ascends to the easy gully above this barrier. As soon as possible gain the rock arête on the left. This is the edge of Striddle Crag, and its clean rough-textured rock is a delight, leading first up an arête, then along a clean ramp to a grassy bay. Move down and right to reach another clean ridge. This takes you to the top of the climbers' crag and the start of the serious scrambling. The buttress steepens and becomes vegetated, but can be climbed by steep heather, first left, then back right, to a small spike belay below a pinnacle. Step down and move right to gain rock then keep to the ridge, mainly on the right-hand side to make best use of the angle of rock. Climb up to easier slopes back left to the top of the steep section. **This is serious, exposed and should be protected by a rope**. The heathery ridge has one more rock step near the top and it emerges at the summit cairn.

The following four scrambles can be linked to provide a good outing in dry conditions.

34. Warnscale Beck

Grade 1 with some avoidable 2✳
NY200136 🛆 ✹✹

Warnscale Head is steep and craggy. The stream drains a wet hollow and needs reasonably low water to make the scramble worthwhile. There are pony tracks on either side of the stream, that on the left being the most obvious.

Approach: From the car park at Gatesgarth go towards Honister Pass for a few yards to where a track branches right into Warnscale Bottoms. Almost level walking gives time to look around at the heathery crags of Haystacks and Striddle, with Green Crag guarding the valley head. Your modest scramble can be seen straight ahead, a stream which bounces merrily over its host rocks.

Route: Start at the first small cascade, topped by a dark green pool. Cross the water-sculpted rock of the streambed to a longer cascade with rock slabs on its

The stream gives an open scramble with a height gain of 300m. Much of the scrambling is easy, on good rock, with escape possible almost anywhere. The rock can be slippery when wet.

Warnscale Beck gives a good scramble below Haystacks

right. Near its top you can continue up easy slabs or make a more sporting step across the flow to a steeper finish. The stream bends left into a defile, best passed easily by rocks on the left. Regain the narrow stream above, duck under a tree and the defile bends right. Cross the slabby right wall by a ledge which peters out. The easiest way is then to step onto a ledge in the water flow and make a few damp moves to reach the lip of the cascade. If there is too much water for this, then the slab is traversed at a higher level with just one delicate step when the holds run out. The right wall is then followed more easily until it opens out.

Above is a broad rock band with the main fall straight ahead. The best scrambling lies near the subsidiary flow to the left, and is reached by a slight descent across the stream. The broad sweep of slabs can be climbed at a rib left of the flow. It steepens near the top; move left (grade 2). Note the U-shaped groove on its right, gouged by the crampons of ice climbers. This makes an entertaining ascent if you are looking for difficulties.

If neither of these routes suit, there are easier options. Just before the streams merge a square-cut recess is passed on the right edge. Continue easily on the left side of the stream to a pool and cascade passed most easily on the right. There is bouldery walking where the stream bends left in a broad ravine. The stream of Green Gully enters on the right. Continue with scrambling here and there. Improving scrambling leads past small cascades – cross to the left wall. There is easier going as the ravine dwindles, then an awkward passage of the left wall to a walking finish past the final fall.

The main pony track lies just to the left. Another track joins here, and a few yards down it on the right is the tiny bothy of Warnscale Head, a renovated quarry hut. More scrambling is found ahead on the rock outcrops around Dubs Bottom. Continue along the main pony track to a grassy hollow in front of quarry spoil heaps. A track goes right to cross the stream and goes below the short rock prow of Little Round How.

35. Little Round How

Grade 2 NY207132

Approach: Follow as described from Warnscale Beck scramble (Route 34), or park at the top of Honister Pass, take the Gable track up the old quarry incline and continue straight over into Dubs Bottom where the rock is just across the stream. A short clean rocky knob rises directly above the path.

Slabby rock requires balance-climbing and dry conditions. Height gain 25m.

Route: Start at the left end from the path and climb easy-angled slabs moving right to the end of a low overlap. Overcome this and mount easier slabs back left to another overlap. Move left below a groove and find good handholds in the slab above to move left onto this. Rocks on the right end in a spiny crest.

Little Round How

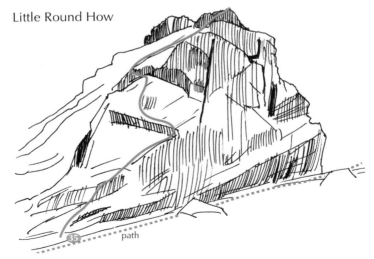

35   path

Little Round How provides a short but entertaining scramble

Directly ahead is big brother, the fort-like wall of Great Round How.

36. Great Round How

Grade 3 *NY206129*

Great Round How

Approach: Follow the path from Little Round How until a short traverse can be made to the right end of the crags.

Route: At the right side of the How is a buttress of clean light-coloured rock, left of a vegetated slabby recess. Start at the foot of the recess and slant up left to a ledge with a steep difficult exit up a corner. More easily again, the route ascends diagonally left to gain a heather ledge. Follow this left and descend slightly to gain a rock shelf, which is crossed easily in an exposed situation to finish up mossy rocks.

Very exposed scrambling on good rock. The crag faces north and is slow drying. Shelving rock is treacherous when wet, so it needs a dry spell to come into condition. The route makes length by following a prominent traversing ledge, tricky to gain. Height gain 50m.

The crux corner at the start of the long traverse on Great Round How

The Coast-to-Coast Path is 50m above past a fence. Here you can go right and descend to reach the scramble on Seavy Knott (Route 32), or go left to join the traversing path from Honister where Route 37 can be used to gain the fell top. Alternatively, gain Moses' Trod to reach scrambling on the Boat Howe Crags of Kirkfell (Route 29).

37. Grey Knotts

Grade 1 NY217128

Easy-angled, not serious scrambling on good rough rock full of holds. The most interesting way needs to be sought after a good start. Height gain 50m.

A modest scramble on the north-west slopes of the fell rises to the summit.

Approach: Park at Honister Pass. Take the Great Gable path which forks left from the quarry road close to the start. After mounting the steep incline a cairned track goes left over the moor to rise gently across the slopes of Grey Knotts. A line of easy-angled crags lie above the path. Your route is on the longest crags directly below the highest point.

Route: Start at a prominent slabby rib. Climb the right side then the edge of the rib past a wrinkled steepening to

Grey Knotts

a neck. Instead of the easy ground ahead walk 5m right to a clean 10m slab. Climb this up its centre to finish up a V-groove. The rib ahead is steep so move right to climb the easy-angled groove. Again, easy ground lies ahead and more fun can be found by going right to clean slabs. Walk to another set of rocks ahead and take the most interesting way to the top.

Scrambling on the rough slabs of Grey Knotts

✳ ✳ ✳

38. Honister Crag

Grade 4✳✳ NY216142

Dark, sombre, inhospitable – this is the first impression given by the north-facing, vegetated buttresses of Honister, riddled with old quarry workings. For the scrambler, the main buttress presents a long challenge with some route-finding problems. This is a **very serious expedition** with an alpine north-wall atmosphere, and is

Honister Crag

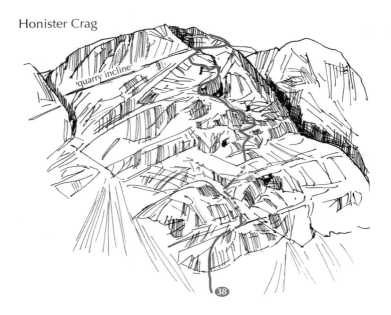

Although surprisingly little rock is encountered, it takes an interesting way up a large buttress, linking easy rocks, intricate sheep tracks and steep vegetation. Slow to dry and inadvisable when wet. **On the exposed pitches a rope is essential for protection. Wear a helmet.** Height gain 320m.

only for experienced mountaineers with good route-finding ability. In the working heyday of the quarries it would have been extremely dangerous to approach the foot of the crags. Now the dangers are less, but there are a lot of loose stones lying on ledges and these could easily be dislodged by sheep.

Approach: From the top of Honister Pass, the crags are best viewed from a lay-by about ½ mile on the Buttermere side, where the road eases in angle, just downhill from the first bridge. There are two main buttresses separated by a central gully (which is best avoided due to the vast amounts of loose material directly above in the old workings). Your route takes the left-hand buttress. Gain the lowest rocks by steep screes.

Vegetation and complex route finding pose problems on Honister Crag

Route: The first section is a slabby buttress, rather vegetated and with a covering of loose stones. Reach the first slanting scree terrace. A short wall of good rock leads to a small curving scree shoot. Take a break on the right, through a steep band, followed by a zigzag course up a broken buttress to gain the edge of a large terrace which slants into the central gully. Above is a broken heathery buttress, which would be most unpleasant to climb if it were not for some tiny sheep tracks which provide an easy zigzag ascent, first right, then back left, then right again. Leave the sheep track where it crosses under a small gully through the heather. The gully is steep and earthy (flake belay on left wall), but it breaks through a steep band to reach a little amphitheatre dominated by a black recess, which from the road appears to be a cave. High on the left skyline is a perched block which is our objective. Leave the amphitheatre by a break on the left and a rocky step to gain a ramp which brings you back to overlook the gully recess. **Rope is advised for the next two pitches.** There is a large belay block at the top of the ramp.

Climb directly up steep vegetation then traverse left via a 'garden' and an awkward exposed rock step (nut runner). Descend slightly to a ledge then up to the perched blocks, stance on top, and arrange a belay with the rope draped under the gun-like rock. Walk along the grass ledge to its end at a slab overlooking the gully. No way here. Return about 2m and ascend two steep heather-topped steps to a sharp rib above. Make a long reach for good holds, and a leftwards swing reaches easy ground on a slanting rake.

From the top of the rake climb under a tree to exit on the old quarry incline. The workings provide interesting rock scenery here, with a tunnel into the mountain. Follow the incline to its demise, overlooking the derelict scene of decaying quarry workings above the central gully. The crazily angled walls of some of these old buildings should be warning not to venture inside. A small path to the left, up a bilberry spur, avoids all difficulties and dangers.

BIRKNESS COMBE

Birkness Combe possesses an impressive array of crags. On the left at the entrance to the combe is High Crag, which merges into the broken mass of Sheepbone Buttress. Further into the combe an array of vegetated buttresses on the left culminate in the impressive flat-topped Eagle Crag. All the crags on this left side face north and are often greasy and unsuitable for scrambling. Facing Eagle Crag are the cleaner easier-angled rocks of Grey Crag, composed of several buttresses perched one above the other. This is a recipe for a great scrambling route.

Harrow Buttress is the first section of the long scramble on Grey Crags

39. Grey Crag

Grade 3✳✳✳ NY172147

This route combines easy rock climbs to create a contin-uous high-grade scramble. **Rope advised for security**.

Approach: Park at Gatesgarth and follow the path round the head of the Buttermere. Start up the Scarth Gap path, but above a wood slant diagonally right on a smaller track to enter the long combe. At its head climb scree to the clean attractive rocks of the scramble high on the right. About 1½hrs approach.

Grey Crag, Birkness Combe, from the approach

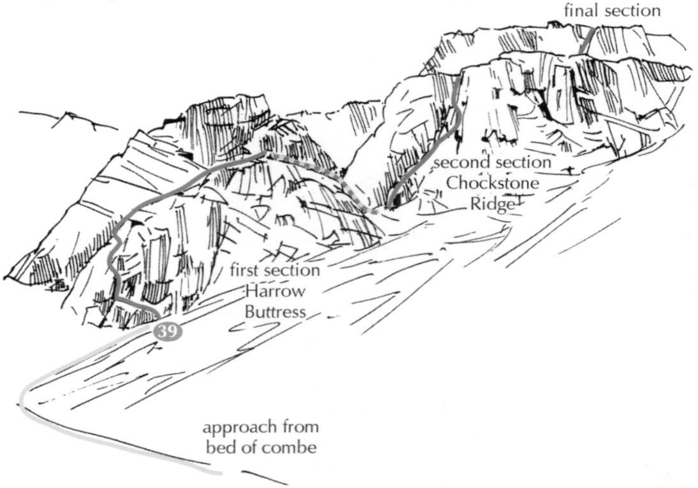

final section

second section
Chockstone
Ridge

first section
Harrow
Buttress

39

approach from
bed of combe

Route

First section: Harrow Buttress

This appears in rock-climbing guides as 'diff', but is no more difficult than Chockstone Ridge. There is a polished direct start up a groove in the nose of the lowest rocks, but an easier way is to traverse a ledge from the right to reach a deep chimney. This is climbed on comfortable holds, facing right, for 7m until an escape can be made to the left on ledges. Climb a cleaned groove on good holds to a platform. Scramble up easier rock towards an

A climber's scramble on good well-used rock, with considerable exposure. Loose blocks on Chockstone Ridge require care. The direct start to Harrow Buttress and chimney finish of Chockstone Ridge nudge the route into a climber's grade of difficulty. Good belays are available. 150m height gain.

Chockstone Ridge

Harrow Buttress, Chockstone Ridge and Final Section

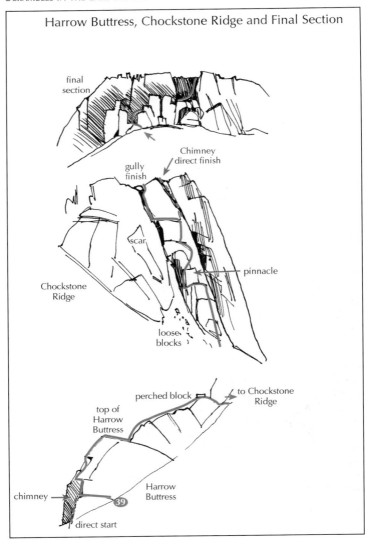

final section

Chimney direct finish

gully finish

scar

pinnacle

Chockstone Ridge

loose blocks

perched block

to Chockstone Ridge

top of Harrow Buttress

chimney

Harrow Buttress

39

direct start

overhang, but about 2m below this move rather awkwardly left into a scoop to reach a rock ridge and the shattered neck at the top of Harrow Buttress. Now follow easy rock ribs and bear right to the best rock, which leads to a huge perched block overlooking the gully on the right. On the face across the gully are steep slabs and to their right is the narrow pillar of Chockstone Ridge.

Second section: Chockstone Ridge

A path descends into the gully to the reach the broken foot of the narrow ridge, which ascends in steep steps, just to the right of an earthy gully. The rock scenery is superb – a mass of towers and buttresses piled one on top of the other. The narrow ridge rears into a pinnacle which can be climbed or bypassed up a short cleft (take care with loose blocks) on its left. From the block at the back of the pinnacle make an exposed move into a groove on the right, where good holds take you back to the crest of the easier ridge. At this point the exposed finishing pitch can be avoided by an escape into the grassy gully on the left to a chockstone, which is turned by a ledge on the right. The more difficult direct finish climbs the steep chimney on good holds but with a rather awkward exit, especially if greasy. A grass platform is reached below the final tier.

Final section

There is a popular 'v diff' climb up the slabby front of the buttress, but a scrambling route is described amidst good rock scenery. The final tier is guarded by large bouldery towers. There is a central recess which seems the logical way, but direct entry is greasy and awkward. Make a long scenic detour to the left to reach the base of the pinnacle blocks and the boulders behind them. Once in the wide recess choose either the grassy walls at the back or the bouldery gully on the right to emerge suddenly on the summit ridge.

✻ ✻ ✻

40. Sourmilk Gill, Buttermere

Grade 2 NY172162 🗻 🌿🌿

The first half of the route climbs open slabs which are very smooth and often covered with a layer of slimy lichen, which is slippery even if ascended in socks. The second half of the route follows an enclosed ravine with short steep steps interspersed with walking. Height gain 320m.

This is the stream which issues from Blaeberry Combe under Red Pike and High Stile. It is very obvious from Buttermere village, where it appears as a continuous cascade on a reddish-tinged bedrock, cutting an open swathe through the adjacent forest.

WARNING

This traditional scramble is an accident black spot. Novice scramblers can easily be tempted by the innocent-looking but holdless slabs into irreversible situations, especially in the usually greasy conditions. Anyone unused to balance-climbing on easy-angled slabs should avoid this route as a slip can result in a long fall. **The route is only suitable for those experienced enough to form their own judgements**.

Approach: The popular lakeside path from Buttermere village goes past the start of the gill near the outlet of the lake.

Route: The first half needs no description – go where fancy takes you and avoid setting foot off the slabs. Above the forest the stream becomes narrower and runs in a small ravine. A steeper cascade is climbed on its left, followed by a short steep wall above a pool – again keep left on large sloping holds. Continue by rock stairways to a steeper cascade climbed awkwardly on its right or more easily in the centre if not awash. A long cascade is started on the right, then cross a pool to finish on the right.

Blaeberry Tarn is not far above and a steep path leads to Red Pike. Further scrambling is easily reached in Birkness Combe of High Stile (Route 39).

41. Hassness Gill, Goat Crag

Grade 1, 2 or 3 NY189161

Above the northern side of Buttermere lake is Goat Crag, deeply riven by a many fingered gill.

Approach: Park at a layby near Hassness where the stream crosses the road. A path leads into the gill.

Route: Where the path leaves the side of the gill, continue up the left bank to enter the ravine proper. Scramble to a

A fairly open gill where one can choose between the slabs of the streambed, if dry, or excursions on the buttress on its right. Height gain 250m.

Hassness Gill, Goat Crag

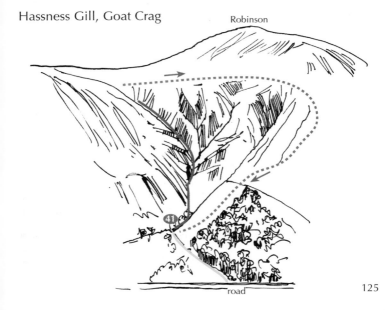

Robinson

road

Hassness Gill

fork at a small reservoir. Keep to the left branch and a rocky defile. This can be difficult in high water, when it is advisable to use the buttress on its right. There are several small falls to surmount. A broader fall can be passed on its left to reach an amphitheatre with a choice of exits. The left branch is the best and runs over slabs that in dry conditions make an excellent way. If it is too wet, scramble up the easy heathery broken buttress between the left and centre streams until the left stream can be regained and followed more easily to a rocky exit.

A descent path is well over to the south-east, past a prominent hollow. Alternatively, a pleasing circuit is over High Snockrigg, where an old path zigzags down to Buttermere village and the lakeside path back to the start.

GRASMOOR

Grasmoor is a massive fell with uniformly steep slopes rising to a gentle swelling summit plateau. The mountain's chief attraction for scramblers is the challenging craggy face of Grasmoor End overlooking Crummock Water. The rocky pyramid is based on a plinth of velvet-smooth grass and rises in a colourful mixture of screes, rock and heather. Splitting the front is the prominent Y-shaped Lorton Gully. A lesser gully to right is Buttermere Gully, bounded by the rocky South-west Ridge, a scrappy scramble. Left of Lorton Gully is the North-west ridge which hosts an enterprising walkers' path.

42. Lorton Gully

Grade 3 ✱✱✱ NY164205 🔺 ⁂

Lorton Gully, Grasmoor

Grasmoor End

There is a short inescapable section with a few steep rock pitches, so the leader at least should have rock-climbing experience, although the difficulties are nowhere great and the situations rarely serious. **Rope advised** in places. Height gain 350m.

A magnificent expedition. Climbers sometimes use this as a wet-day epic when they can frighten themselves on the slippery shelving rock. Scramblers must choose dry conditions, when the watercourse virtually disappears, to enjoy the ascent to the full.

Approach: There is ample parking at Lanthwaite Green on the unfenced road below the gully. A path starts up the grass, well to the left of the obvious cleft, then slants diagonally right across the scree cone into a little dell below the gully.

Route: Mount clean rock shelves to gain the narrow heathery gully trench. The first part is unusual, as it

The deep gash of Lorton Gully splits Grasmoor End

follows a clean narrow rock bed surrounded sometimes by head-high heather and juniper, which stout people may find constricting. Scramble up the rock staircase to a bay with trees above. The exit is steep with good finishing holds. The next rise is topped by a holly. Reach this, first by a square chimney, then a slab to the steep wall below the tree. This is climbed easily by a direct ascent to slide effortlessly between trunks and emerge in a bilberry bay. Now it is mainly walking up the strip to enter a narrow defile which is the crux of the route. The character changes to a more serious inescapable gully rising in a series of steep little steps between narrow walls. The first step is easy, then there is a 5m chimney best climbed by straddling. Above, a 6m step to a ledge and an easier step ends the testing section.

Ahead is an amphitheatre, with easy escapes at each side, backed by a steep rock wall. This is where the gullies split. Entry to the right-hand gully is barred by a steep red corner which is not a scrambler's route. You take the left-hand gully, which starts just above the rock barrier, about 30m left of the red corner. Start up the wall to gain a left-slanting ramp to a ledge. Climb the mossy wall above on good holds to enter the V-shaped gully which rises in entertaining rock steps and culminates in a steep finish, avoidable on the left.

There is easier going now, although a shallow V-groove slows progress. The gully forks, the left branch having most rock, then merges again to continue with little further interest. It is time to leave the gully for more entertaining but shattered rocks of the ridge on the left. This joins the North-west Ridge path at a tower.

Continue along the ridge path to the summit plateau, where a fine walking circuit is around the head of Gasgale Gill, over Hopegill Head and the rocky ridge of Whiteside back to Lanthwaite Green. Alternatively the path down the North-west Ridge is a direct rapid descent through improbable terrain.

NEWLANDS

The Newlands valley lies parallel and west of Derwentwater, biting into the fells in a spectacular valley head. The eastern wall is a mass of crags, yet they are unsuitable for good scrambling. There is a lot of loose rock and steep heather. Whilst scrambles have been recorded, they are best left for the intrepid explorer. At the head of the valley Dale Head Pillar does provide a route. There is car parking by the river at Littletown.

43. Dale Head Pillar

Grade 1✷ NY226157

Dale Head Pillar

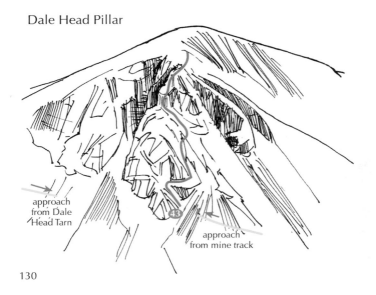

approach
from Dale
Head Tarn

43

approach
from mine track

This crag of greasy, slow-drying rock guards the head of the dale. It has a sombre atmosphere but provides good rock scenery.

Approach: From Braithwaite or Portinscale follow signs to Stair then Littletown. Park at the bridge just before Newlands church. Walk back up the road 30m to a path which joins the mine road up the dale. Go along this past the flat-topped knoll of Castle Nook. Ignore the left fork, cross the stream and gain height on the old zigzag mine track until well right of the Pillar, whence a traverse can be made to the lower buttresses. An alternative approach is from the col at the valley head – useful if approaching over High Spy from the Knitting Haws scramble (Route 47). From Dale Head Tarn traverse a craggy hillside by a tenuous sheep track, the line of which should be ascertained on the way.

Route: On the right toe of the buttress is a grass rake leading left. After 30m, at a small rowan, take a grass ledge right to another rowan. Ascend rocks behind this, traverse a slab to the right and emerge onto easy ground. Unsatisfactory rocks on the edge can be followed for a while, but recourse to the easy ground on the right has to be made. This steepens, but an easy line leads back left across rock and heather to the edge. This develops almost into a path, then pleasant scrambling follows up broken rocks with dramatic drops into the gully on the left. There are good views across to Eel Crags.

A broad buttress which narrows at its top, where it comes close to an impressive vertical drop into the gully on its left. It is dark and greasy, and care is required. There is almost a path in the upper half. Height gain 140m.

Newlands Valley with Dale Head Pillar at its head

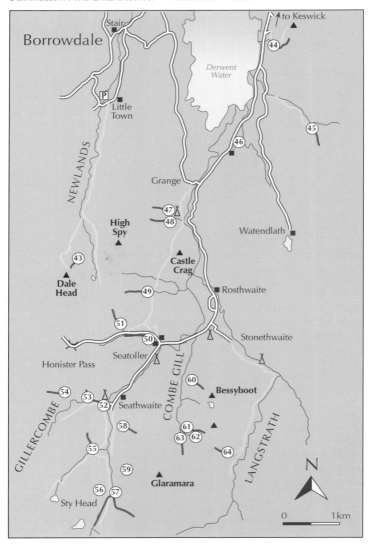

Borrowdale

to Keswick

Stair

44

Derwent Water

45

P

Little Town

NEWLANDS

46

Grange

47

High Spy

48

Watendlath

43

Castle Crag

Dale Head

49

Rosthwaite

51

Stonethwaite

50

Seatoller

Honister Pass

COMBE GILL

60

Bessyboot

54

53

52

Seathwaite

GILLERCOMBE

58

LANGSTRATH

55

61

63 62

64

59

56 57

Glaramara

N

Sty Head

0   1km

BORROWDALE

Renowned for its gentle beauty, Borrowdale and its satellite valleys have much to offer the scrambler, with a good choice of quality routes to suit varying weather conditions. As a centre for exploring neighbouring valleys and fells, it can hardly be surpassed. Styhead and Grains Gill give access to the Scafell and Gable area, whilst a short drive brings Honister, Buttermere, Newlands and Thirlmere within easy reach. Rock quality varies in Borrowdale. In places it is equal to the best of the southern Lakes; in others it is smoother and more friable. There are campsites at The Hollows (Grange), Rosthwaite, Stonethwaite, Seatoller and Seathwaite.

Car parking and transport

There are car parks at various points in the valley, but these quickly fill at busy times. Even so, you should manage if you are prepared to walk a little further.

A good bus service, the Borrowdale Rambler, runs from Keswick to Seatoller, where the last bus back leaves at 9pm (except Sunday).

44. Cat Gill

*Grade 1** NY272210* 🔺 ✿✿

Less than 2 miles south of Keswick, Walla Crag is the first of the rocky, forested bastions which so characterize the eastern bounds of Derwentwater. Hidden from view is a delightful gill which curls around the southern edge of the wooded hillside. This narrow rocky gill catches the afternoon sun, and provides a scramble in beautiful surroundings. It is also a popular geological excursion, as the succession of rock beds are well seen. The water catchment area is not large and so the trip is feasible fairly soon after rain has run off.

The rock is sound and not too slippery. A path lies close to the gill and escape is possible at all times. Seek the most interesting rock close to the water for best sport. Height gain 150m.

Scrambling in Cat Gill

Approach: From the National Trust Great Wood car park in the woods below Walla Crag, take the path signed 'Ashness Bridge' to a footbridge at the base of the gill.

Route: The gill is interesting from the start, a pretty, narrow little rock trench with scrambling–walking. Climb a little fall to cross the path, then traverse a rock shelf on the right wall. An awkward exit is best achieved by crouching low. A footpath comes close to the gill; ignore this, and stay with the rocky bed past a narrow awkward fall. The gill bends to the left, with some steep little steps, then narrows into a V-trench with a slabby left wall. Interest is maintained with traverses across little pools and innocent-looking but awkward ascents which could be quite wetting if there is too much water flow. A change of character follows with more open rock steps to a final steep wall. Exit on the left or, if there is not much water in the gill, the steep left wall can be ascended athletically by a quartz band. After two more short steps the gill emerges onto the moor.

The summit of Walla Crag is a short way to the north-east, a fine viewpoint. The return path by the side of the gill is well graded and provides an easy descent.

45. Ashness Gill

Grade 4✱✱✱ NY277193 🔺 🌿🌿

A fine expedition for the enthusiast who likes the liveliness of a good wet gill. It was once described briefly in a rock-climbing guide as 'A historical curiosity for those who like that sort of thing!', and was first climbed in 1924 by Archer Thompson and his Italian guide Angelo Dibona. The route calls for rock-climbing experience in the party, as it is more a waterfall climb than a typical Lakeland gill. It is enjoyable in fairly dry conditions, but waterproofs are advised. Technically the climbing standard is only moderate, but the rocks can be very greasy, and recourse to an ascent in socks may be wise.

Approach: Park just above Ashness Bridge on the Watendlath road from Borrowdale. This is a popular tourist attraction for its picture-postcard views. A path on the right of the stream leads up the hillside to the obvious ravine. Enter the stream below this.

Route: A preliminary cascade provides an aperitif before the main ravine is reached at a junction. Scramble up a rock rib in the right-hand branch to a pool, traverse this on the right and climb an easy staircase on the left of the first cascade. Oak belay on the left. The next section looks impressive. Traverse right on ledges to the edge of the stream, move up a little (good nut runner) then traverse across the spray and up to a platform on the other side with no satisfactory belay. Ascend steep rocks on the right of the stream to another ledge well above and a tree which is awkward to reach but could provide a belay. Traverse left into the narrow streambed above the

Lack of good protection and the length of the main pitch make it a serious but enjoyable trip. **Rope advised** and a steady leader. High water would render the upper third problematic and retreat nasty. Height gain 70m.

cascades. There is a small nut belay low on the left of a pool below another short steep fall. Climb this and exit right onto wide ledges. The final cascade, if too wet to climb direct, is avoided by the right wall. A sting in the tail.

46. Jackdaw Ridge, Shepherd's Crag

Grade 2✳✳ NY263184

Jackdaw Ridge, Shepherd's Crag

descent gully

Although Shepherd's Crag is a very popular rock climbing crag it has one offering of interest to the scrambler. The crag nestles amongst the woods immediately above the road between the Lodore and Borrowdale Hotels. The ridge has proved a popular introduction to roped rock climbing for many youngsters.

Approach: There is no adequate parking nearby. Climbers often use the limited parking offered to customers of the High Lodore Farm cafe at the south end of the crags. Alternatively the bus from Keswick stops at either of the hotels. A path behind the farm leads over a stile into the woods below the crag. Jackdaw Ridge is 10m further on where the path abuts a steep rock wall.

Route: Start at the left end of the steep rock wall close to vegetation, where a tree sprouts from the back of a rock flake. Start behind the tree and climb steeply on large holds to a ledge, followed by another steep wall to a larger ledge with a tree. Climb a corner on the right to another ledge. At the point of arrival step left from a rock onto an easy ramp slanting right to a large tree. (Further right is very easy ground that can be approached from the descent gully just over the stile and gives an easier but less interesting grade 1 scramble this way.) Above the large tree is a tricky-looking groove with a steep exit right on good holds onto easy terrain. This can be avoided by a detour to the right. A delightful spiked ridge is followed to a neck at the side of a steep wall. Go right and ascend a groove behind a large tree to the flat vantage point at the top of the crag.

A path leads into the adjacent descent gully through the trees to the south.

A spiky ridge, with a steep start. Every hold is a comforting jug handle. The scramble incorporates the bulk of the ridge and ends at a flat belvedere with fine views. Height gain 70m.

47. Nitting Haws

Grade 2✱ NY247168

A mix of easy scrambling and walking. Some shattered rock requires care. Height gain 260m.

Rising above the woods, which so attractively clothe the valley floor south of Grange, is a turreted spur. This is on the west side of the valley close to the famous narrowing of 'The Jaws' and lies to the right of the steep sombre-shadowed wall of Goat Crag. The spur makes a fine grandstand overlooking one of the most attractive parts of Borrowdale.

Approach: There is a tiny car park by the bridge at Grange and another small parking area on the main road well before the bridge; alternatively, use the Borrowdale Rambler bus from Keswick. Another option is to park at the Bowderstone car park further down the main road and wade across the river (when the water is low) to reach The Hollows. From Grange follow a lane signed Hollows Farm. Before the farm a left fork leads to the river and the

Nitting Haws

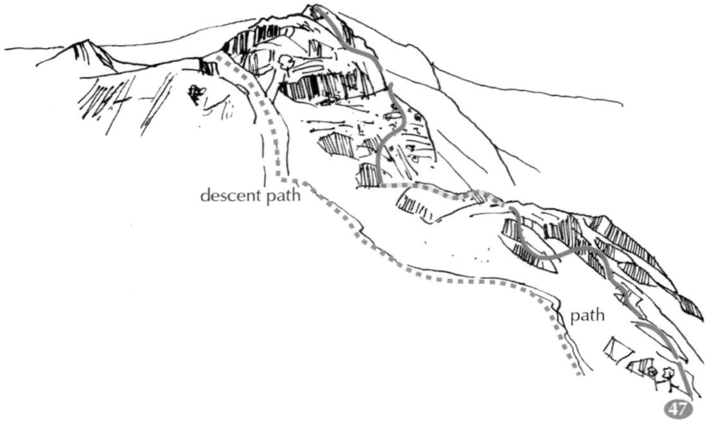

descent path

path

47

camping area. Note that only campers are allowed to drive here. Go right, through the main camping field to a stile onto the open fell. Cross to the first rock slabs on the right at a group of trees.

Route: Start at the first rock slabs on the right of the trees, with very easy scrambling on rock amidst the bracken slopes to a steeper outcrop. Climb a nice little rock rib on the right to a terrace below a steep band of rocks. Walk horizontally left to a grass terrace above a holly and continue to another holly at the foot of a ramp at the left side of the steep rock wall. Climb the ramp past another holly to a break in the right wall. Go up this to the top. There is a section of rocky hummocks to cross before the hillside steepens again. The first hummock is climbed on its steep front by a rightward-slanting ledge; then go back left to easier ground.

The buttress now rises in a slope of juniper-covered rocks, with three spurs separated by scree. On the left is a clean little nose. Climb this just left of a hawthorn at a right-slanting groove. Climb the front of the nose above on good holds. Now you are on a shelf below another steep wall which does not offer a scrambler's route, so cross the scree to the right to a rocky spur. Wind a way up this amongst the juniper, up left above a holly, then cross a smooth slab on the left side into juniper forest to another slab and boulder field, slightly right. Climb this slab, trending right, then keep to the crest of the spur to a grass terrace below the steep upper wall. Walk right into a recess to the right of a holly. A groove above this slants left to the top of the steep band, and a track leads through heather to the foot of the next rocks. There is a rowan at the right end. Climb just left of the tree, bear right up a heather ramp then left at a break to nice rocks on the crest. Climb direct up the next nose and an easy slab to the summit.

The scramble on Dale Head (Route 43) can be gained by a walk over High Spy. Alternatively, a path starting between the top of Nitting Haws and Gate Gill descends close to the spur.

48. Gate Gill

*Grade 2, 3 or 4*** NY247167* ⚠ ❧

A solid slabby rock bed for much of the way, but the smooth rock is slippery when wet. Socks over trainers could be useful in greasy conditions, and a **rope is handy** to safeguard difficult key sections. Varied and continuous scrambling culminates in a striking ravine in good situations. Height gain 270m.

An entertaining trip up the watercourse between Goat Crag and Nitting Haws. The gill carries a lot of water in spate and dwindles to a trickle in a dry spell. Gate Gill is unnamed on the OS maps, but has been known by that name locally for generations. The local name for Goat Crag is 'Gate Crag'.

Approach: See Route 47. The main camping field of The Hollows has a stile at its top which gives access to the fell. Mount a steep path which bears left to join the stream just above the woods.

Route: Start at a tree-lined defile and mount an over-hanging block by the stream. On the right wall is a broad slab over which the stream cascades in ribbons. Start at the bottom right and go diagonally left across the water to a small tree. Follow slabs through a V-shaped channel to a boiler plate slab on easy ground. Walk to the next interest where the stream cascades over a series of stepped slabs climbed on their drier right. Enter a wet recess and climb the middle of this, through a second wet opening.

The excellent scrambling continues – go below a holly and climb the steep wall just left. A chaos of large boulders leads into a verdant defile between steep walls, where the way is blocked by an unclimbable cascade over smooth rocks. A way is possible up the mossy rocks on the right (grade 3). Start up a very slippery slab, where knees prove useful, to reach a tree. A groove slants left above, with good holds over its right edge. There is an easy alternative to this pitch by a grassy ramp on the left.

Regain the stream immediately and climb a crack just right of the water. A stretch of boulder scrambling ends at a large block with mossy slabs on the right. Climb these past the block. The ravine becomes very impressive where a branch stream enters in a thin fall down the

Scrambling in Gate Gill

almost vertical right wall. Continue up the main stream ravine by a steep central rib which curls up to a tree below a smooth cascade. Cross an exposed ramp 6m to the right, then work back left on good ledges to the top of the fall. The next cascade presents a serious obstacle in all but bone-dry conditions, but is easily bypassed on the left.

Pass a short steep barrier and cross left to below an overhanging side-wall where flakes lead right into the base of a cascade which fills a black cleft. This presents a serious climax (grade 4), but is rarely in condition. The cleft is very wet, greasy and about 20m high. Climb the first section by holds on the right wall until you can bridge to reach a spray-filled platform. The final fall necessitates a steep ascent hampered by the water. Note that there are no belays on this pitch – it needs a very steady leader and a rope for the rest of the party. Avoid this fall by the juniper slope on the right and regain the stream above.

There is a little more scrambling – pass another unclimbable fall by ledges on the right wall, then climb a broken cascade. The stream flattens out in a craggy heathery basin below High Spy, and several rock outcrops can provide amusement if you are heading for the tops.

There is a steep descent path close to the gill, on its north side.

49. Scaleclose Gill

Grade 1 or 2 ✳ *NY243146* 🔺 🌿🌿

Good rock and interesting scrambling after a feeble start. A narrow gill, only worthwhile in a dry spell. Steep parts are short (about 3–5m), although some steps are quite tricky in places. Height gain 230m.

The slopes of High Scawdel are not easily noticed by the traveller in Borrowdale. They lie hidden from the casual glance behind wooded lower knolls, and only a keen eye sees the deep-cut narrow gill biting into a craggy bracken-covered hillside.

Approach: The shortest approach is from the car park at Seatoller, although the path from Grange, behind Castle Crag, also leads to the gill. At the end of the car park, cross a stile and walk directly uphill to reach the old bridleway. Zigzag upwards on this, but where it heads towards Honister cut right to a gate on the open fell. Follow the path right, over a low col, and continue to a footbridge over the gill.

Route: Gain the gill above a wall. A black waterslide above a little pool hints at things to come. As usual in this type of scramble, keep close to the water for the best sport – you can easily miss the good bits. There is a succession of rock steps as the stream passes the first crags, then a change of character – a narrow defile. Gain the defile, straddle the pool and make a damp ascent of the narrows – good scrambling! It continues with interest; cross a wire fence and mount steep little rock steps in the gill bed. The angle relents as the side-walls open, but the walls soon close in again and the scramble again becomes full of character. A fall is awkward to surmount on the right and

The first obstacle in Scaleclose Gill

143

leads to another tricky step, passed direct using the left wall. Round a bend a narrow cascade may be passable in dry conditions. Avoid it by a side channel on the right and regain the gill above. The difficulties are not over yet. There is an awkward two-step rock band, which demands neat footwork near the stream, and finally another narrow defile before the moor is reached.

There is a straightforward descent near the gill on its south side, or cross the moor to reach the scramble on Dale Head Pillar (Route 43) at the head of the Newlands valley.

50. Hause Gill, Seatoller
*Grade 1** NY244138* 🏃

The most accessible gill scramble in the Lake District is popular with outdoor and adventure centres as an introduction to the delights of the sport. The route is entertaining and full of variety.

Parallel to the road with numerous escapes, the route runs in a succession of cascades and little ravines, where progress is often made by traversing the rock bed above pools. Height gain 110m.

Approach: Park at Seatoller or use the Keswick Rambler bus. Enter the stream just above the village on the Honister Pass road.

Route: Boulder walking leads to a cascade in a succession of steps. The small ravine opens where many paths arrive at popular summer bathing spots. A fall below a rampart of the road is passed most easily on the left. Boulder walking takes you to the next ravine, with an interesting traverse on the right wall close to the water, then join the stream to finish. A side-stream enters on the left. Just before this follow an overflow channel on the right, or you can stay on the right of the main stream. A succession of twisting cascades gives fun if you stick to the rock bed. A deep pool appears to be a serious obstacle but a traverse on the left wall has been cleaned.

The ravine ends where the stream cascades at several points over the steep left wall. The easiest way is just right of the left cluster of cascades, where a short mossy wall has been cleaned. The more open stream above continues to give good sport if the narrow rock bed is followed to exit on the moor close to the cattle grid.

Tricky moves above a deep pool in Hause Gill

Route 51 is close – on the right just above the wall end.

51. High Scawdell Gill

Grade 1 or 2 ✳ *NY236142* 🔺

A pleasant scramble up a short narrow rocky gill on the slopes of High Scawdell above the Honister Pass road. It makes an entertaining diversion to fill an odd hour or to do after Hause Gill, as it is so accessible, faces south and has excellent rock. This is one of several gills in the area first ascended by A. R. Thompson and Angelo Dibona in

Clean rock in a narrow bed, with cascades, chutes and many small steps to surmount. Height gain 70m.

1924. Thompson, who lived in Keswick, was a keen gill scrambler and sometimes, as in this case, was accompanied by his alpine guide.

Approach: There are parking places on the roadside where the gradient eases after the stiff pull out of Seatoller towards Honister Pass. The gill is seen on the right above the intake wall. It cuts a small ravine through crags in its upper part.

Route: The way is obvious, and the two major difficulties, climbable in dry conditions, can both be easily bypassed on the left.

The following three routes combine to make one of the most popular scrambles in the Lake District, and for the very fit there is further scrambling on Great Gable or Kirkfell.

52. Sourmilk Gill, Borrowdale

Grade 1, 2 or 3★★★ NY233122 🏔

The rock is excellent and the situations picturesque and interesting. The broad slabs of the main cascades offer a variety of ways that are all good. Height gain 210m.

This makes a fine prelude to a day on the higher fells. It is an accessible open gill, with escape possible anywhere by simply moving away from the rocky bed.

Approach: Park at Seathwaite, turn right at the farm under the barn arch, go over the footbridge and the gill is straight ahead.

Route: A path leads into the gill – a bouldery walk at first – to the first small fall passed by a slab on its right. More bouldery bed leads to a steeper section, where a cascade falls into a beautiful greeny pool. Climb the rocks on the right then, where the stream runs over broad slippery slabs, keep to the dry rib on the right which runs into attractive slabs. The longest sweep of slabs is a swathe of

The left side of the main cascade in
Sourmilk Gill gives a grade 3 scramble

foaming water in wet conditions and a thin water ribbon in drier weather. The most difficult scrambling, if the water allows, is on the left; the easiest and more usual is on the right, where pleasing slabs offer a variety of choice. At the top of this section regain the stream and keep to the best rocks. A small fall is avoided on the left, then climb a dry central rib to reach an amphitheatre with a striking pinnacle. The stream cascades down a square recess. Climb the steep left-hand rib to a rowan, then a gangway on the exposed edge runs to the lip of the cascade to exit abruptly on the moor.

On the right, just over a stone wall and stile, is the long low wall of Seathwaite Upper Slabs.

53. Seathwaite Upper Slabs

Grade 1 or 3✳ NY228123

A broad belt of slabs of excellent rock. Height gain 20m.

Approach: From the top of Sourmilk Gill cross the stile in the wall on the right to face the slabs.

Route: The easiest lines follow cracks with the most positive holds, but the slabs can be climbed anywhere. The smoothness soon gives a feeling of exposure, and you need to stay calm on small holds. The best ways take the longest most continuous sweep of slab; the easiest is a little way left, starting just left of a grassy groove and finishing by a crack.

From the knoll above the slabs you can see the next scramble on Gillercombe Crag (Route 54).

Seathwaite Upper Slabs give good balance climbing

54. Gillercombe Crag, North-East Buttress (Rabbit's Trod)

Grade 2✱✱✱ *NY223125*

The large rambling buttress of Gillercombe Crag dominates the right-hand side of the combe. It contains a number of classic rock climbs on the front of the

Gillercombe Crag

fence

buttress and this popular scramble which incorporates the easy-angled rocks on the right edge.

Approach: Best by way of Sourmilk Gill (Route 52) and Seathwaite Slabs (Route 53), although a path on the left of the gill also zigzags into the base of the combe. From the top of Seathwaite Slabs cross the moor towards the crag. Keep left of a large boulder to pass the wall then go right over a fence to screes below a gully. Mount to the foot of the slabs at the base of the gully on its right. This descends from the right end of a grass terrace two-thirds of the way up the cliff.

Route: On the right of large screes the lowest slabs provide a preliminary scramble. Walk left to a slabby rib which is the right wall of the gully. Climb the slabs following a well-trodden way, interspersed with heather, to a rock ledge where you traverse left towards the gully. Mount more slabs to a recess, exited on the left to a shoulder below a slightly steeper section. On the more shelving steeper rocks above take care to find the easiest

A good mountaineering route – first up slabs, where the best way keeps to the rock rather than the steep adjacent grass, then up more broken but steeper steps in the upper part. Escape is possible at several places. **It is best undertaken in dry conditions, as the slabs become difficult and serious if damp.** Height gain 160m.

On the slabs of Gillercombe Crag

151

route, which goes at first almost into the gully, then back right before moving up left on ledges to reach the level of the big grass terrace below steep rock. The tapering slabby rib above leads into the more broken upper buttress. Ledges go right into scrappy terrain, but to the right of a fierce little crack climb a short break in the steep wall to a ledge. Keep on the airy left edge to where it steepens into cracks one above the other. Do not be tempted to ascend these unless you want a genuine rock-climbing pitch, for the second crack is steeper and more awkward than it appears – and retreat is not easy. Instead, from the foot of the cracks traverse right and climb a steep little corner from a comforting ledge. Move towards the airy left edge above and finish nicely up rough grey rocks.

Note

This route incorporates the bulk of 'Rabbit's Trod', described by Bentley Beetham in his guide to rock climbing in Borrowdale in 1953. Beetham discovered a large number of rock climbs and scrambles in the area, many designed for taking youngsters into adventurous situations. Current rock guide books have discarded many of his inventions, but some such as Intake Ridge and Cam Crag Ridge are now classic scrambles.

55. Base Brown from Taylor Gill Force

Grade 2 or 3 ✱ *NY230110*

A long scramble with a sting in its tail that finds a way up a craggy hillside. It is very easy to stray into difficulties, although climbers will relish opportunities for more difficult direct pitches up the ribs of the higher crags. There are fine views down Borrowdale and over Sty Head.

Approach: Park at Seathwaite. Take the path right at the farm, under the arch, to cross the stream. Follow a track up the valley towards Taylor Gill Force. Where the waterfall comes into view, the main path crosses the crag to a gate. Below this are slabs. Descend from the path to the foot of the slabs.

Route: Climb the lowest rocks 10m right of a holly. At the level of the tree traverse left below a block to a grass ledge. The rocks ahead are mossy and more difficult, and they are best avoided by going right to reach the path. Immediately through the gate is a deep chimney-groove. This is steep but has good holds, and a nut runner can be arranged at the crucial exit. From the ledge above mount a steep wall onto easier-angled rocks at the top of the first

After a steep start the route is open to variation, but a rock band which guards the top makes a fine finish. The rock is generally very sound, although mossy in places. On the exposed sections **a rope is advised**. There is some steep rough walking between crags. Height gain 280m.

Base Brown

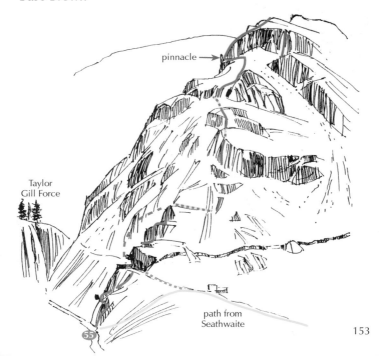

pinnacle →

Taylor
Gill Force

path from
Seathwaite

Outcrops of good rock are linked on the Base Brown scramble

section. (If the deep chimney-groove is too greasy, this can be avoided by continuing 50m up the scrambly path to traverse right on grass ledges below a large holly at the first major break in the crag. This brings you to the top of the first section.)

There is now a wide choice of routes, and the following is just one. Walk to the short rib on the right, with a cluster of spikes near its foot. Climb the pleasant slabby rib. Walk to the foot of prominent rocks above. Climb the left flank of the spur on good holds, moving right at the top. The next steep little barrier is composed of loose blocks. Take care! Climb the left end then zigzag up.

Ahead is a more serious obstacle – a buttress of steep rock which offers scope for direct rock-climbing pitches. The easy way avoids the steep lower rocks by walking left past a juniper patch and up a grassy gully until easy slabs are accessible to the right. Climb these rightwards to the top of a knoll. Another crag barrier lies above, and the easiest route is not obvious. Climbers can make a direct way up the clean spur straight ahead, which steepens at its top, but the easier way described is full of character. On the left is a pinnacle at the foot of a skyline ridge. Walk to gain a ledge which runs above the pinnacle. Just before the edge belay on a small tree. Climb up past the tree and across a nasty earthy heathery scoop to a ledge on the exposed rib. Climb it, bearing left to a large shelf. Difficulties are now over as easier rocks lead to the top of the spur. The summit of Base Brown is still a plod ahead.

The best descent is from the col towards Green Gable, where the path into Gillercombe is joined. Further scrambling on Kirkfell can be reached by going over Green Gable into Wind Gap, where a traverse path below the Gable Crags reaches Beck Head. The traverse path continues with a slight descent to the foot of Boat Howe, East Buttress (Route 29). This, followed by a traverse of Great Gable and return via Sty Head, makes a great day out.

56. Ruddy Gill

*Grade 1 or 2** NY235099* 🏔 🌿🌿

Grains Gill is the valley which forms the head of Borrowdale past Seathwaite and runs high into the fells below Great End. A popular walkers' path en route for Scafell Pike runs up the valley, crossing Ruddy Gill near its foot and keeping it close company as it leads to a wide grass shelf under the crags of Great End. This scramble is best tackled in a dry spell, as in places the ravine is narrow and thus impassable in any but low water conditions.

Each of three distinct sections gives good scrambling on clean rough rock. Nowhere is the route serious, even in the final ravine, as it is always easy to escape. However some of the individual passages are quite awkward. Height gain 500m includes walking.

Approach: From Seathwaite, follow the stony track up the valley to Stockley Bridge. Turn left after this and continue up the valley past a wall. Then, after a derelict wall, leave the path to join the stream and enter a small ravine.

155

Route

First section

Follow the main ravine of Grains Gill for a short way to where Ruddy Gill enters over the steep right side-wall. This is your route, and a rock staircase on the right of the cascade makes a good start. Broad slabs follow to a pool guarding the entrance to a narrow rock trench which closely holds the stream in a string of deep green pools

Water-worn smooth rock in Grains Gill

and lively cascades. Traverse the guardian pool on its left wall to reach a more difficult pool. It is possible to traverse the difficult steep left wall, but it can be avoided by climbing out of the gill and re-entering just above the cascade. Easy scrambling in the delightful watery trough ends at the footbridge where the main path crosses.

Second section

There is walking for a while past easy slabs in the streambed to a slight narrows with a slabby cascade at its back, which is climbed on the right; then cross the water to finish up slabs on the left. An easier stretch follows over the attractive rock bed past pools and a slabby cascade to another narrows. Enter this by its left wall and continue close to the stream. A deep pool within steep side-walls presents an awkward problem unless you wade, which is contrary to the spirit of the game. It is possible to cross dry shod by the left wall in low water to reach the slabby back cascade. Bypass the next steep fall to end this entertaining section.

Third section

The upper ravine is some distance away and it is best to join the path for a while. Enter the ravine where a small side-stream joins on the left. More enclosed, and between higher walls, the surroundings assume a more oppressive air. A double cascade is passed by slabs on the right wall, and the next fall is avoided by grass ledges on the right. The bed is broader now, and a cascade is climbed close to the right side. A sentinel central boulder is passed either side to reach a circular pool. The next part is quite tricky, but an escape can be made from here if required. Pass through a portal to a narrow pool where a cascade bars exit. Climb the steep right wall for a metre or so. A hidden foothold above the pool aids the awkward start, then cross carefully left to easier ground. The leader can protect the followers from a ducking with a rope slung over a tree above. There is a final pool, which can be passed on its left wall by the determined or avoided by means of a chicken run and escape up a gravely furrow on the right, which ends abruptly on the shelf below the impressive crags of Great End.

A great scrambling day can be achieved by going over the nearby Esk Hause, dropping down into the head of Eskdale to the Cockly Pike Ridge of Ill Crag (Route 117, vol. 1) or (for the really fit) the more difficult South-West Face of Ill Crag (Route 116, vol. 1).

57. Grains Gill and Allen Crags

*Grade 1 or 2*** NY235099* 🌿🌿

At the head of Grains Gill, well left of the path, the hill-side is cut by a prominent V-shaped ravine amidst a number of isolated crags. The ascent of Grains Gill followed by a way linking the crags gives a sporting approach to the fell top. This is a varied expedition, with the contrast of splendid gill scrambling amidst great beauty and the more open exposed rocks of the crags.

Approach: As Ruddy Gill (Route 56).

Route

First section
The ravine is broad and bouldery at first. Pass the incoming cascade of Ruddy Gill and continue up the much diminished watercourse in the narrower ravine. Use a mossy ledge on the left wall and pass a large jammed block on its left. Note an old mine trial just before a sharp bend in the stream. The water flows down a thin quartz vein which is climbed to a succession of little rock steps which end this entertaining grade 1 section.

Middle section
There is a stretch of walking close to the stream. Head for the crags, split by the narrow deep ravines in the shape

of a V. The scrambling begins again about 50m past two prominent trees, where the main stream bends to the left. Clean rock in the streambed gives a long stretch of continuous open scrambling into the jaws of the ravine. An ascent of the ravine is difficult and only feasible in very dry conditions. Leave the ravine at its entrance by rocks on its left wall to reach grass slopes bordering its left side. Rocky ribs and slabs are then linked to avoid most of the grass until the gully on the right can be crossed at a grassy bay and a horizontal sheep track below the main buttress on the right.

Top section
On the right of the bay, the track goes below a steep rib. Start just left of this, climb a leftward-slanting heathery

Although the crags are not difficult, sound judgement is needed and **it is advisable to take rope**. It is possible, but less interesting, to avoid the crags. Best done in a dry spell. Height gain 370m includes walking.

Grains Gill and Allen Crags

57

In the lower section of Grains Gill

groove, then come back right to reach easier-angled rock on the crest. Climb the rough rocks with care, for there are some loose blocks and the exposure is considerable. Pass a vertical step by traversing a ledge on the right for 3m to reach a vertical break ascended on large holds with care in order to regain the crest. An impressive prow looms ahead, but an easy way is found on diagonally rising ledges just round the corner on its left. About 15m from the base, a ledge runs right onto the edge in an exposed position above the vertical prow. Easy scrambling along the spine merges into rock walking. Finish the route in enterprising style up the final cluster of rocks on the left.

A walk over Glaramara makes a logical return.

The steep western slopes of Glaramara host several rocky streams, two of which provide undistinguished scrambles.

58. Hind Gill

Grade 1 or 2 NY239116

Lies close to Seathwaite just north of Hind Crag. A very steep path runs by the side of the ravine, providing a popular descent from the tops.

Approach: Park at Seathwaite, and take the main valley path for ¼ mile to below the gill, where a gate gives access to the fell. Zig-zag to the intake gate on a faint path and drop left into the base of a ravine.

Route: The gill is long, but scrambling is limited to the lower half. Much of the trip is over boulders and is lacking in character.

The north-west aspect of the ravine encourages mossy rocks. In poor conditions the rock is slippery, and the grade quickly becomes 2 with more than a trickle of water.

59. Red Beck

Grade 4 NY238103 🌲🌲

This is for the connoisseur – interesting if you have the judgement to safely overcome friable rock and steep grass.

The side-walls of this picturesque narrow gill are brecciated and thus inherently shattered.

Approach: From Seathwaite take the path up the valley, past Stockley Bridge. After 2km cross Grains Gill at a footbridge. Zig-zag up the steep hillside to reach the ravine of Red Beck.

Route: There are five steep cascades before the gill fizzles out into boulders. **Rope advised**. The gill is only feasible in a dry spell.

Red Beck will only appeal to the connoisseur!

COMBE GILL

This valley joins Borrowdale between Rosthwaite and Seatoller and has plenty to delight the scrambler. It is at a low enough altitude to be worthwhile when higher fells are cloud covered. It is possible to combine routes into a long scrambling expedition.

60. Intake Ridge

Grade 3 ✱✱✱ *NY253128*

Intake Ridge

glaciated slab

A number of outcrops can be linked to make a good scramble, with some entertaining sections on very good rock, **some of which may need a rope**. Height gain 200m.

This was first climbed in 1937 by Bentley Beetham, who introduced many youngsters to the sport. The Glaciated Slab hosts several easy rock climbs, some of which could be added to the day's sport.

Approach: A narrow lane opposite Mountain View, signed Thorneythwaite, has parking on the right after 200m. Return along the lane a short way to where a path on the right mounts through woods to a wall at the entrance to the open fell. Intake Ridge starts across the stream where the wall runs into the first rocks. An alternative approach starts from parking on the broad roadside

The exposed crossing of Glaciated Slab on Intake Ridge

verge near Stonethwaite school. A path goes from the church and through Church House farm. Take a left fork to traverse into Combe Gill on the left side of the valley.

Route: Start at the lowest point of the rock spur close to the wall. Ascend a cleft and easy-angled rock to grass where a descent slightly right gains a longer spur. Climb the clean front of this on a well-used way at first by a steep wall just left of the nose, then by easier slabs towards a cluster of small trees. 6m below these take a gangway left to easy ground. Climb 6m of broken rocks then walk right to a corner with a slab. Climb this rightwards to a well-worn platform on the edge of **Glaciated Slab**. (You can avoid this next difficult part by traversing left onto easier ground.)

The next section is exposed, although it is easier than it looks. **Rope advised**. From the platform traverse right on a foot ledge which leads onto the smooth exposed slab. Move up a short crack to better handholds and easier-angled rock on the crest of the slab. Place a nut to protect the second from a big swing. There is a metal-spike belay on the grass platform.

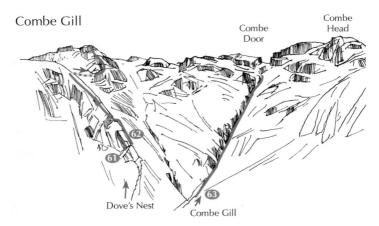

Combe Gill

Combe Door

Combe Head

Dove's Nest

Combe Gill

Gain a very easy spur on the left, which in turn gains a better buttress above and slightly left. Climb a heathery trough just right of the sharp nose of the buttress, starting by a rock rib on its right. At the top of the trough escape up the heathery left wall on big holds, and go left at the top to easy ground and another series of easy rock ribs. At the foot of a steeper section is a grass platform. Do not attempt to climb the steep rocks directly above, but follow a terrace to the right. Just before the edge climb up steeply, just left of a jutting nose. From the ledge above traverse the fine slab to the right edge and easy ground. Another group of rocks can be incorporated on the way to the summit.

Make a slanting descent into Combe Gill to reach Route 61 on Dove's Nest Crag.

61. Dove's Nest Crag, The Attic Cave
Grade 2✱✱ NY253116

A strenuous trip into the Attic Cave – more a window than a genuine cave. This is a short scramble of variety and interest on comforting holds amongst steep rock. You come back down the same way. 20m height gain.

Dove's Nest Crag is a fine clean buttress, formed by a large rock slip that has left huge slabs leaning against the rock face with cavities behind them. Gravitational forces are still active here, and a once popular exploration of the caves was deemed dangerously unstable some years ago. The described route still seems OK, but changes may occur.

Approach: Paths starting near Mountain View lead into the moraine-filled combe (described in the approach to Route 60). Ignore the rising path on the right and continue up the valley floor until below the crag on the left. Walk up the right-hand side of the crag, which is eroded at its base. 20m up from the base a well-marked trod leads left into a cleft in the crags.

Route: The path goes to the foot of a cleft. There is a huge gap where a large rock has peeled from the parent crag.

Dove's Nest Crag

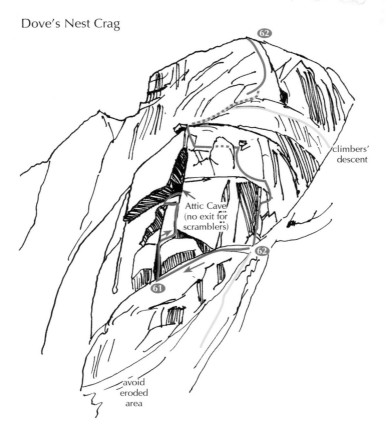

Go round the front of this to a chimney at its far left end. Climb deeply into this, up a strenuous 3m, wondering at the apparent ferocities above, to discover an easy squirm under a large chockstone to a balcony on the other side. (This was the entry point of the infamous Rathole, a tight and strenuous but now dangerously unstable caving trip.) Traverse the balcony left and step into a V-groove capped by an overhang. At its top escape right onto a platform below a capstone. Clamber over boulders and through a hole to reach the balcony of Attic Cave. This is as far as you go and it has been great fun. Do not worry too much about descending the same way – it proves easier and less strenuous than the ascent. **A rope is useful for the nervous.**

The logical continuation is by Route 62.

62. Dove's Nest
Crag, Right-Hand Groove

Grade 3 ✷✷ *NY253116*

An exposed step on the steep lower crag demands **rope protection**, then easier-angled scrambling on knobbly rock takes you to the summit ridge. Height gain 140m.

Approach: As for Attic Cave (Route 61), go 20m up the right-hand side of the crags, where the ledge traverses across the front of the crags. If you have done the Attic Cave route you will have returned to this point.

Route: Scramble easily up a corner to a scree ledge. Climb a steep corner on excellent holds then move right to a flake. Go up this and a little right again. Ascend easily 5m, then make an easy traverse left across heathery grooves to reach a good rock platform. A staircase leads on then right by a rowan, back left up a groove and round the back of a detached block. Continue left along the tip of the narrowing block and make just one very exposed move from its end on good holds to reach the top of the main crag. **Rope advised.**

There is a climbers' descent path on the right, but a long stretch of good scrambling remains and it would be a pity to abandon the route. Three slabby steps are ascended on superb rough knobbly rock. Either gain a further stretch of rock on the left to the summit or (better) at the top of these slabs walk across a grassy slope to the right to reach an easy-angled slabby buttress. This gives an additional long delightful scramble up the now familiar perfect volcanic ash to the ridge.

A walk along the ridge to the right leads to Combe Door, the nick at the top of Combe Gill. The rocks of **Combe Head** can be scrambled – at first by descending slightly on the Combe Gill side to a slabby break in the steep wall. As a final flourish there are the summit rocks of **Glaramara** across a grassy basin. A return by the main path along the western arm of Combe Gill, above Raven Crag, makes a good day.

63. Combe Gill

Grade 4✳ NY251114

This is the deep-cut ravine at the valley head. It is more oppressively gully-like than most Lakeland gills.

Approach: As for Routes 60 and 61 – the ravine is obvious past Dove's Nest Crag.

Route: A steep mossy fall is passed by the grassy right wall. Two lesser cascades are followed by a black repulsive cave pitch. Retrace steps to the foot of the cascades, where an escape on the right wall goes out of the gill, but a traverse across steep grass regains it. The next obstacle is a short fall with a flat capstone. Go under the capstone and exit strenuously on the right wall. The next cascade is damp even after a prolonged dry spell (a steep escape is possible below this on the right wall). Climb the first part of the next fall by the left wall to a boulder perch under a huge block. Make a difficult exposed move to gain a gangway on the right wall, which is climbed on unsound rock.

Easy bouldery sections are interspersed with fierce little cave pitches, only feasible in dry conditions. Unsound rock and few escapes make this a serious trip. **Waterproofs and rope are advised**. Height gain 220m.

LANGSTRATH

As the name implies, this is a long valley, which joins Borrowdale at Stonethwaite. It hosts one of the area's most popular scrambles, a great way onto the fell top.

64. Cam Crag Ridge

Grade 1, 2 or 3✳✳✳ *NY262110*

Another of Bentley Beetham's 'climbs' which have achieved popularity as a scramble.

Approach: There is plenty of vergeside parking along the lane to Stonethwaite and limited parking in the hamlet. Only campers can drive further. Either go along the rough lane past the campsite or take a riverside path through the meadows. The lane bends below the prow of Eagle Crag and rises into the broad strath of the upper valley. Walk past Sergeant Crag on the left. At a gate note the landmark boulder of Blea Rock on the other side of the stream. Just

Cam Crag Ridge

past Blackmoss Pot, a popular bathing spot in a small ravine, you will see Cam Crag on the right. A path slants through bracken to its base. 1hr approach.

Route: The path goes round a boulder field and leads onto the rocks of the lowest spur. Good well-worn holds lead up right then back left and more steeply up to the top of the first part. Walk across to the broad buttress ahead. The best scrambling follows a succession of diagonal cracks or grooves close to its right edge. The first crack steepens into a short vertical corner which is more difficult (grade 3) than anything else on the route, but has good holds. The grade 2 way avoids it by moving left just below the steep corner and up a wall on good holds. At the next step climb the left of two cracks, moving right at the top. Higher, a right-slanting crack is easier than it looks. The rock changes to a smoother texture but is still nice to climb. A series of short slabby walls are conquered to the top of spur.

Once on the hummocky ridge, you could cross it and descend into Combe Gill for scrambles on Dove's Nest Crag (Routes 61 and 62) or walk to Glaramara. A shorter return lies over the scrambly craggy top of Rosthwaite Cam to Tarn at Leaves and Bessyboot. Just beyond this a path descends Stanger Gill. This develops into a made stone track which goes directly to the Stonethwaite campsite.

After the initial section the route is a buttress edge rather than a ridge. Difficulties close to the right edge can be easily minimised or avoided by keeping left. The excellent clean solid rock is a delight to climb. Height gain 200m.

Cam Crag Ridge gives splendid scrambling

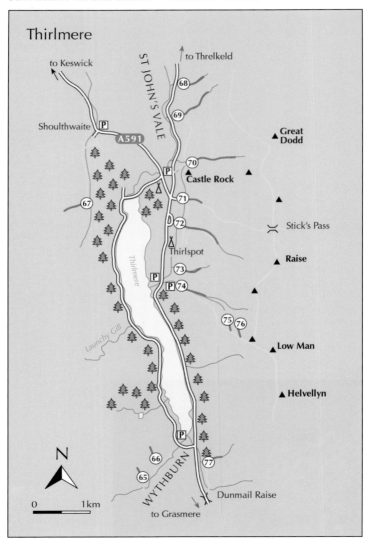

Thirlmere

to Keswick

ST JOHN'S VALE

to Threlkeld

68

69

Shoulthwaite

P

A591

70

Castle Rock

Great Dodd

71

Thirlmere

72

Stick's Pass

67

Thirlspot

Raise

73

P

P 74

75 76

Launchy Gill

Low Man

Helvellyn

P

N

66

65

77

WYTHBURN

Dunmail Raise

0   1km

to Grasmere

THIRLMERE AND ST JOHN'S VALE

Dark plantations surround Thirlmere, where unnatural tidemarks betray the water's prime function – it is used primarily for drinking water. Its former unfriendly aspect has diminished with the opening of forest trails and an abundance of picnic and parking places by the narrow road along its western shore. However, the landowners, United Utilities, **discourage gill scrambling**, particularly in the western forest, and ban it around Armboth and Launchy Gill – important SSSIs. The eastern side of the valley is a long unbroken sweep of fell stretching from Dollywaggon Pike and Helvellyn to the Dodds. The lower half of this hillside falls steeply and is cut by gills which can be used as a livelier means of gaining height up an otherwise dull hillside. St John's Vale is a peaceful haven away from the bustle of through traffic which swings away towards Keswick. Rock quality and texture vary. There are campsites at Dale Bottom, High Bridgend, Thirlspot and several closer to Threlkeld and Keswick.

Car parking and transport
Thirlmere is well supplied with car parks. There is a regular bus service between Keswick and Windermere.

WYTHBURN

Wythburn is a deep valley which runs into the head of Thirlmere. Nab Crags form the rocky western side of the valley. There are several scrambling possibilities on the broken rocks of this extensive craggy hillside. Take care with loose flakes.

65. Nab Crags, South Buttress

Grade 3✷ NY312120

Better than it looks, on rough rock; it improves after the first scrappy bit. Height gain 80m.

Approach: Use Steel End car park, on the narrow lane which runs around the western side of Thirlmere, close to the head of the lake. Opposite the car park, take a permissive path which runs close to the river. As you pass below the skyline edge of crag, your easier-angled rocks are seen just beyond. Turn up the hillside just before a gap in the wall before the footbridge. Cross a fence in a higher wall and zigzag steeply up to the lowest rocks.

Route: Start at the lowest rocks. A horizontal grass ledge leads right to the edge of a broken rock buttress where a trodden way unfolds up walls, slabs and ledges. A steep corner is the crux fairly low down, perhaps worth grade 3. At a large terrace with boulders move right and take a leftward-slanting edge. Short walls complete the ascent to the fell top.

South Buttress, Nab Crags

For a pleasant descent walk along the edge of the crags northwards, past a prominent cairn, to reach an old track just before a wall. Descend right to the road at Stenkin, close to the car park.

66. Nab Crags, Perched Block Route

Grade 2 NY314126

An easy-angled buttress offers the most continuous route in the centre of the crags.

Approach: From Steel End car park follow the permissive path by the streamside up Wythburn. Pass below the buttress, which can be identified by a sweep of slabs trending slightly rightwards. At the third stile, turn uphill by the wall. Go through a gate above the turn of the wall and make a way tortuously over a steep slope of bracken and rocks diagonally right to the foot of the slabs.

After a messy start up vegetated rock the scramble improves. The pitch past the perched block makes the route worthwhile. Height gain 80m.

Perched Block Route, Nab Crags

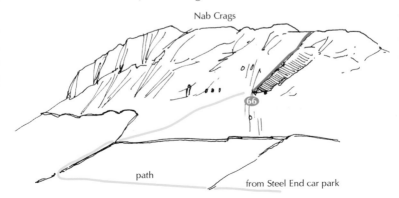

Nab Crags

66

path

from Steel End car park

Route: Start at a rib on the left side of the buttress at a tiny tree. Climb the rib with care on steep earthy rock. The next section is easier on better rock – straight up the left side of slabs to a large terrace below a steep wall capped by overhangs. Note the perched block which juts above. Go round the left side to a groove which allows easy access to a ledge which traverses the buttress above the overhangs to reach the perched block. This is a very exposed pitch but is surprisingly easy. More slabs are climbed to the top of the buttress. On the left are two steep slabs which can be climbed to the ridge. The first slab is traversed diagonally left to right to finish up a crack.

The edge of the crags is an attractive place with fine views over Thirlmere and St John's Vale. Descent can be made down the little valley at the back. At a flat shelf below a stone beacon on the ridge, an old pony track is joined, which zigzags down to Stenkin.

The western side of Thirlmere is densely forested and cut by several gills which are now out of bounds to scramblers, as they are the domain of rare plants. This includes **Launchy Gill**, a difficult scramble, rarely in condition, now an SSSI, and **Middlesteads Gill**.

67. Mere Gill, Shoulthwaite

Grade 3 ✱ *NY298188*

The Shoulthwaite Valley is one of those quiet little Lakeland gems bypassed by the majority of walkers. It leads to nowhere in particular, and though there are imposing crags the rock attracts few climbers. If this gill is not bone dry it must be ascended in socks over footwear, for the rock – although rough – is slippery, especially where it is black. Use of trainers with socks over the top transforms the holds from impossibly slippery to reasonable.

Approach: The valley lies behind forested slopes above the northern end of Thirlmere and is approached via Shoulthwaite Farm. A private lane leaves the A591 opposite a loop of old road which is now reserved for parking, although supposedly there is a 2hr limit. There is room for parking at the end of the farm lane, but permission is required. A track goes left through the farm buildings and enters the forest. Double back right on a forest road, and where the angle eases a path forks right through a gate to cross the stream and join the right-of-way path up the valley. Walk well past the beetling Iron Crag to reach Mere Gill, which is an unmistakable rocky defile.

Route: There is an introductory section below where the path crosses the gill. To do this, go down the path to enter a ravine in the main stream. Above the path there is a delicate move almost immediately, on the left wall, then step into the watercourse. The black cascade above is steep and slippery. Cross the pool at its foot and keep close under a bulging wall on the right of the cascade until forced to ascend steeply on good holds. Above, climb rocks near the left edge with a steeper finish onto an opening in the ravine. Another ravine beckons ahead. Mount the first waterslide slabs on the left (quite tricky), then cross right into the ravine. Ascend the right wall by a gangway.

Whilst the difficulties are short, the general nature of the scramble puts it at the top of its grade. **A rope could be useful** in places for those unfamiliar with scrambling in socks. Height gain 110m.

Mere Gill has some short difficult steps

The good scrambling continues – a steep wall is ascended, then easier rocks to a pool passed on the right under trees. It is worth continuing up the narrower defile ahead, which gives sporting scrambling to a final steep wall.

The excursion can be followed by a stroll along an upland shelf to the right above Iron Crag, with grandstand views of the full length of the Dodds to Helvellyn, which from this angle appears to possess a graceful summit cone.

68. Sandbed Gill

Grade 4∗∗∗ NY319217 🔺 🌿🌿

St John's Vale has a steep mountainside forming its eastern flank, with several streams cutting their way through the crags. One stream bites much deeper into the mountain than the others – this is Sandbed Gill. Penetrating the hidden recesses of this ravine is a unique expedition which was first accomplished by the Abraham brothers in 1890. To safely undertake this trip it is wise to have a

Sandbed Gill

Fisher Wife Rake

Bram Crag quarry

68

An inescapable adventure amongst luxuriant vegetation and slippery rock with the crux right at the top. **Rope, waterproofs, spare socks and a dry spell advised**. The ravine has a very steep right-hand wall, with the left at a more amenable angle; most of the scrambling utilises this factor. The cleanest rock lies close to the stream, but it is extremely slippery and great care must be taken. Height gain 300m.

leader with rock-climbing experience, although only two or three short pitches can be considered climbing. The rest is enjoyable scrambling. The exit pitch is best climbed in socks, which give a better grip on the sloping holds.

Approach: There is a parking place near the southern end of Bram Crag Quarry. The road into the quarry has a 'No footpath' sign, but only a few yards up this road at the bend the open fell can be gained above the intake wall and a traverse made to the foot of the gill. A direct way across the field also leads to the gill. Alternative parking at Legburthwaite car park allows a return walk over the Dodds.

Route: Enter the narrowing ravine at a large tree and proceed easily at first amongst luxuriant flora, which includes foxgloves, juniper and nettles. Having negotiated these hazards an interesting section follows up the narrow watercourse, with two small rocky steps to a major obstacle in the form of a steep, greasy fall which is climbable in very dry conditions. It can be bypassed on the left wall by a series of ledgy steps (or an exposed scramble further left) then steep grass to an overhung recess. Reach the shelf above either to the right or above the overhang. Follow this shelf down and across an exposed scramble to regain the bed of the gill.

Back in the stream another waterfall is more easily avoided by a short rock pitch on the left (awkward to start). Traverse back into the stream and enjoy an interesting wet section where the streambed narrows in its rocky confines and is capped by a large chockstone, bypassed damply on the left. The climax of the expedition is a forbidding waterfall with a slippery-looking ramp on its left. This is a genuine rock-climbing pitch of about 9m which will usually be treacherously slippery due to the nature of the rock. Tackled in the conventional way it would be testing, but the crafty will remove boots and proceed much more securely in stockinged feet. A rope and competent leader is advised. Note that a falling second may swing into the waterfall. If the flow allows, some leaders prefer to battle directly up the bed of the fall. The gill opens above into an amphitheatre, and whilst the scramble can be continued to the bitter end it is as well to end here.

Descent can be made with care down the grassy ramps and slopes amongst the crags just to the north of the gill, but study the diagram beforehand to identify the best route. Further north is the easier but unpleasantly stony Fisher Wife Rake. Bram Crag quarries need to be avoided. A much better continuation is to finish by a traverse of the Dodds along the smooth grassy fell tops to Sticks Pass, which gives an easy descent to Stanah and Legburthwaite.

69. Beckthorns Gill

Grade 3 ✳ *NY321210*

About ½ mile south of Sandbed Gill, another stream is less deeply cut into the hillside than Sandbed Gill, but it creates an interesting scenic ascent at an easier standard than its illustrious neighbour. This expedition involves a lot of easy scrambling, one difficult pitch and some fine ravine scenery. The watercourse is quite narrow, and an ascent is only feasible in dry weather.

Approach: There is no direct right of access to the gills on this side of St John's Vale. Perhaps the best way is to traverse above the intake wall from the base of Sandbed Gill (Route 68); or, if coming from Legburthwaite car park, continue above the intake wall past the base of Mill Gill (Route 70).

Route: A steep little wall gives access to a V-trench with slabby rocks on its left side. Scramble easily up the gill, mainly by its slabby left side, keeping to the rock as much as possible, and head up through a picturesque little ravine. The gill twists among juniper, gorse and trees. Above a steeper cascade, the ravine is more deeply cut.

Out of the streambed the side-walls are shattered and contain a lot of loose scree (**care required**). It is similar in some ways to Sandbed Gill, but easier and less serious, for it is always easy to escape. **The rock is treacherously slippery where wet** – use footholds on dry rock wherever possible and climb the crucial pitch in socks. Height gain 340m.

The bed is narrow and mossy, so take to slabs on its left wall, taking care on fine scree. Regain the gill, which is safer than the loose side-wall, and ascend a short slippery narrow stretch to a circular pool. Scramble up the grassy left wall and regain the stream at the head of a cascade. Pass the next fall on the left and return to the gill by a rock break.

Now a series of steps leads to the major obstacle – a thin mossy cascade with no easy bypass. This is the crucial pitch and is best climbed roped with a steady leader. Footholds in the watercourse must be used, and socks are advised for a secure grip. Climb the first part on the left of the water then use mossy ledges in the stream for a few moves to regain the left side. Ascend a few feet then transfer awkwardly across to a channel on the right which leads easily to the top.

Walk up the now easy-angled ravine to another mossy cascade, climbed damply in its bed. The ravine is easier now amidst striking rock scenery. There are a number of small cascades to surmount, and a side-stream enters down the crags on the right. A steep little fall in a defile is bypassed by a steep loose traverse of the left wall. At this point the good scrambling is over and escape can be made (right) to easy slopes.

The gill expedition continues for those who want to carry on to the bitter end or make a way to the tops. Do not follow the ravine, which culminates in an impassable fall, but take to the left wall, carefully, on scree and rock ledges above the steep drop into the gill. The rocks are shattered and the scree unstable. Regain the haven of the gill, which peters out below the flat grassy ridge of the fell top.

A walk along the smooth grassy tops of the Dodds is a pleasing continuation to gain Sticks Pass for the return to the valley. Alternatively an old grass track zigzags down the steep slopes just south of the gill to regain the intake wall.

70. Mill Gill, St John's Vale

Grade 4✳✳✳ NY321198 🌿🌿

Tucked into the steep hillside left and behind Castle Rock is this superb gill. The base of the gill lies on United Utilities land, and the company does not encourage scrambling. To enjoy the expedition you need a dry period. The entry pitch soon becomes impossible and other pitches are unpleasantly hazardous in all but low water. In a dry spell all the falls except one are feasible direct.

Approach: Park at Legburthwaite pay car park a short way along the St John's Vale lane from Stanah on the A591. Follow the path marked Castle Rock, cross the road and go up steps to a steep path. At a broader cross path turn left along this. Just before it goes into the wood go right to a stile and footbridge over the water leat. 30m above, cross a fenced gap between boulders and go along the wall-side to reach the gill. Alternative free parking is at

A splendid succession of incidents in a rocky ravine. Some of the wet mossy rock is slippery, and a popular solution is to use trainers with socks over the top where necessary. **A rope is advised** to safeguard several steep pitches. Height gain 200m.

Avoiding a deep pool in Mill Gill

Stanah, by the junction with the A591. This is useful if you intend to return by the Sticks Pass.

Route: Enter the dark verdant recesses of the narrow ravine to climb the right side of a short fall. If you can surmount this dry, then the route should be feasible. Not far ahead is an unclimbable fall clenched between steep smooth rocky walls. Exit on the right, using a series of steps and ledges. Regain the bed of the gill easily at the top of the fall. The next mossy cascade is bypassed on the right wall. Cross the slippery rocks at the top of the cascade and continue in a rock trough to a widening. A deep pool is passed on its left. Ignore the right-hand branch of the gill and keep in the main stream, which swings left to ease in angle. By keeping to the rocks of its left wall a sporting traverse ends in a long stride onto a perched block.

A tamer section follows where the gill cuts through the easier-angled slopes level with the top of Castle Rock. The walls close in as the next ravine is entered, and easy scrambling past several small cascades leads to a deep little pool defended by steep walls. Either make a tricky traverse of the left wall or wade into the pool until it is possible to bridge up the cascade at its back. Ahead, a waterfall shoots over a broad steep barrier. Reach its foot by slabs on the right wall then climb a central rib to the barrier. Cross the right-hand flow to climb the steep right wall on good holds. The good scrambling goes on in a succession of little cascades and falls. Enter a narrowing awkwardly and bridge damply up the next fall. Keep on the right wall past the next fall, with a steep awkward exposed little wall at the top, to reach an arched block. You can pass this on its left or do a caving through-route.

The most continuous scrambling is now over, but interesting hazards still appear. There is a steep tricky cascade – start on the left then step across to ascend the right wall. The next fall is rounded on the left. Another cascade by the left side of a huge jutting block is climbed on its left, entered by a delicate traverse. Alternatively, avoid it by climbing much higher. The rocks to the right of the fall are insecure blocks. The next cascade has slabs on the left and nettles to finish.

Still it goes on, with a cascade over green mossy rock – start on the left and go behind a detached block to gain slabs above. The gill appears to be finished, yet there is a tricky traverse of a right wall and an ascent of two cascades before it finally fizzles out.

The grassy crest of the Dodds provides an easy way back over Great Dodd, Watson's Dodd and Stybarrow Dodd to reach Sticks Pass, where a right turn will take you back to Stanah.

71. Stanah Gill

Grade 1 NY321189 🌲🌲

This slight ravine makes a more interesting start to Sticks Pass. The only difficulty can be easily avoided.

Approach: Park at Stanah, the junction of the St John's Vale lane B5322 with the A591. Follow the signs 'Sticks Pass' to a stile at a water leat. Directly above this is a rock knoll which forms an appetizer to the scramble. Where the path crosses the gill take to the streambed.

Route: The first cascade is passed by a shelf on its left, then a short walk leads to a more serious obstacle in a deep-cut verdant ravine. This is climbed by a slab rising from the pool right of the fall and is difficult for 4m before the streambed can be regained. A mix of walking and mild scrambling culminates in two fine waterslides – the first passed by a gangway on the left, the second direct in dry conditions. Soon the stream changes character and runs in an attractive bed, then there is more walking to a final cascade over boulders. Escape to gain the track on the right.

A disjointed ravine with easy escapes. The general angle is not steep; the rock is quite good, and the ascent pleasant enough. Height gain 250m, mainly walking.

72. Fisher Gill

Grade 2 ✶ *NY319183*

An attractive gill rising in a succession of cascades and falls in a shallow twisting ravine. The main waterfalls are impassable but add to the scene. **Take care on the slippery rock.** Height gain 200m.

This gill tumbles down the steep lower slopes of Helvellyn in a rocky bed with a succession of waterfalls, waterslides, pools and runnels. The first part is hidden in a plantation, and only the upper falls are visible from the main road.

Approach: Turn off the A591 400m north of the King's Head Inn at a lane to Fisher Place, where it is possible to park. Follow waymarks past cottages to a stile at the start

Socks make the ascent of slippery rocks less hazardous in Fisher Gill

of the plantation. Walk left to reach the dry bed of the gill (the water is captured by an aqueduct a little higher).

Route: The narrow rocky ravine gives a good start with a steep rise to the concrete aqueduct. Leap across or walk 50m to a footbridge. Now you have the stream to contend with, and it falls into the aqueduct down a two-step slab climbed on the left by a smooth ramp. There is easier walking in the more open streambed amidst larches to cascades – the first easily passed; the third in a steep walled ravine. Enter this from the right, and cross the mossy left of a portal to a basin below a narrow fall with a jammed stone. Climb easy rocks on the right.

The next short ravine is only passable in drought so regain the stream above at a sharp bend. Pass under a footbridge. The stream twists in a narrow slippery rock channel best conquered in socks. We are on the open fell, with the stream in its private ravine twisting to reveal a fine waterfall. Gain the base of the fall by a rising traverse along the right wall, then cross to an easy-angled rib which leads out of the gill. Re-entry is possible above a holly. In dry conditions this fall can be climbed by continuing up the right-hand rocks until they steepen; step left into the fall (socks) and ascend mossy rocks in the water.

A stretch of interesting scrambling in the narrowing stream ends at an awkward cascade. If the water is low it is possible to ascend in the streambed to easier ground and a wide basin. If too high, escape onto the left side of the gill and walk up the edge. You are at the upper falls, a spectacular waterspout which shoots over a vertical cliff. The gill can be followed occasionally for a short distance, but unless the water is very low it is best to view this section from a walk up the side. Above the main falls you can regain the stream and find a little scrambling before abandoning the now gentle valley for the adjacent path on the right.

Brown Cove Crags (Routes 75 and 76) can be reached for more scrambling.

73. Whiteside Gill

Grade 1, 2 or 3 NY318172 🌾🌾

Slippery where wet or mossy. Too much water fills the available rock. Height gain 130m.

A slight scramble up an insignificant gill provides a little interest on the way to Brown Cove. This narrow stream is noticeable in flood, when a continuous white ribbon cascades over rocks. In drought it almost dries out, and makes a reasonably interesting scramble which offers more rock than the adjacent Helvellyn Gill.

Approach: Park at the Swirls car park below Helvellyn Gill or the free parking over the road. Cross the stream and take the path left signed 'Sticks Pass'. Leave the main track at another sign to go left above the intake wall. Round the first spur reach a footbridge over a stream.

Route: Start in a little ravine above the bridge, up left of a fall, then straddle the narrow watercourse. Above is the crux, where a tree guards access to a dark recess. Creep into the recess and, if the water allows, climb the steep narrow wet cleft at the back (grade 3). The other alternatives are all shattered, so avoid the difficulty on the right. More amenable scrambling leads on. At a split in the stream the right channel offers most sport, with small rock steps and slabs which culminate in a steeper barrier. Climb 3m right of the fall to gain a shelf with a steep finish. The rocks peter out above.

Continue up the steep hillside to join a path which contours right into the base of the combe below Brown Cove Crags.

74. Helvellyn Gill

Grade 1 NY320167 🌿

Approach: Park at Swirls car park halfway along the eastern side of Thirlmere or at the free parking over the road. This is the start of a popular path up Helvellyn.

Route: Small cascades in a rocky bed lead to a more impressive cascade with a smooth slab climbed on its left. Keep close to the streambed with its pools, waterslides and rock ribs, mainly walking to a short steep fall climbed in its wet left corner. Pass a jammed boulder and a

A scenic route towards Helvellyn with a little scrambling here and there. The rock is slippery when wet. Height gain 200m.

One of the few rocky bits in Helvellyn Gill

cascade above damply on the left. Stay with the stream, although the scrambling is over, to reach the combe below Brown Cove Crags.

There is good scrambling for the competent in Brown Cove. Alternatively, the path to Helvellyn mounts the right-hand edge of the crags.

75. Stepped Ridge, Brown Cove Crags

Grade 2✳ NY331159

Approach: By either Whiteside or Helvellyn gills, or by the main tourist track up Helvellyn from Swirls car park. At a broken wall continue directly into the combe, where the rocks appear on the right. Right of the main Central Buttress is a gully, and Stepped Ridge forms its right edge.

Route: The foot of the ridge has a steep defensive barrier with rock-climbing possibilities. The original scrambling

Stepped Ridge, Brown Cove Crags

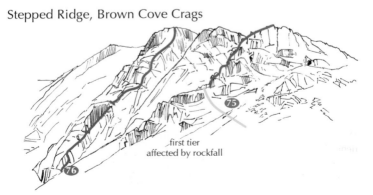

first tier
affected by rockfall

route has been damaged by rockfall and thus it is probably best to avoid the lowest tiers and gain the broad easier-angled ridge above at a shelving grassy terrace.

Continue up the broad ridge, most interesting close to the steep left edge which drops into the bounding gully. Keep left on a rock shelf overlooking the gully, then move back right to the top of an easy-angled slab – take care with some perched blocks! Move left again to an airy platform overlooking the edge and make a tricky exposed ascent onto the easier ridge above – a fine pitch on superb rough rock.

The next problem lies at a narrow neck with a steep wall above. Step down left, clasp an upright flake and mount carefully over a bunch of perched flakes to gain the ridge crest above. From the right climb shelves close to the left edge. At 6m, faced with a smooth slab, move right to a grass ledge. Regain the ridge. At the next rise cross a delicate slab left and step down to a ledge round the corner on the edge of the void. Make a steep ascent – take care with loose flakes. Step from a sharp block to continue along the ridge. Pass through a block barrier to another block rib. Climb the left side of this to emerge on the top.

The path to Helvellyn follows the crag edge, and if you intend scrambling again in Brown Cove it is best to descend this path until you can easily traverse into the combe.

An easy-angled broad ridge with steep steps of rough grey rock. Some loose flakes and perched blocks demand judgement. Scrappy at first, it develops into a fine ridge where most difficulties can be avoided. Height gain 120m.

76. Central Buttress, Brown Cove Crags

Grade 3 ✱✱ *NY332159*

The main buttress makes a fine way to the tops for experienced scramblers. Route-finding skills and general competence are required, as the atmosphere is one of seriousness – although the difficulties are not too great. For maximum interest the described route is

Central Buttress, Brown Cove Crags

A long scramble which takes the challenge of a direct route up the main crags. It includes the best rocks of a broad broken buttress. The rock is generally good, though there are shattered holds in places and it is slippery when damp. Height gain 150m.

recommended, although many scramblers take a different route every time they visit.

Approach: From Swirls car park, halfway along the eastern side of Thirlmere, either scramble up Helvellyn Gill (Route 74) or take the laid track which zigzags up its right flank until a traverse can be made into the combe after a ruined wall is reached.

Route: In the centre of the crags is an obvious buttress, longer than the others, with a broad terraced base. On its right edge a sweep of clean rocks rises to a narrowing rib which culminates about 60m from the base, just to the right of a prominent corner crack. Your route takes this rib then breaks through the steep wall above by a unique and intriguing hole.

Start about 20m up the right-hand side of the buttress at a left-slanting gangway below a steep wall. A small cairn marks the start. Climb the gangway leftwards then come back right across a slab below the steep rocks to enter a grassy groove. Climb this steeply to a shelf below another steep wall. Follow the shelf left to a recess at the left side of the now easier-angled rib. Gain the rib on the right and scramble to its end in a grassy gully. Do not follow this if you want maximum rock – instead walk along an exposed narrow rock ledge on the left onto the front of the buttress, where easy scrambling arrives at a balcony, along with the grassy gully if preferred.

Above is a jumble of crag in a steep wall which seems to offer no way. Grass rakes slant right and left. Take the right-hand rake to where it ends below a steep rock tower. On the right the rib is composed of perched blocks. Go along a grass ledge to the right side of these then climb a crack on the left which leads into a corner at the side of the impressive tower. Escape seems improbable, but in the corner is 'Riley's Window', through which it is possible to crawl to conquer the steep band. A solo scrambler with a bulky rucksack could have problems here and would need a hauling rope.

Scramble to the foot of deep crack in a block above, then move into a recess on its right to twin grooves. Begin

Emerging from Riley's Window on Brown Cove Crags

up the right groove then cross into the left to finish. Walk up the grass rake above for about 18m to a large boulder. Cross flaky ledges to the shattered rib on the right. Climb this for 4m then cross the grassy gully on the right to a block at the foot of a quartz-speckled ridge. This is very shattered, and it is probably best to go further right before scrambling cautiously diagonally rightwards on slightly better rock. A final stretch of easy rocks leads to a grass ridge which links onto the parent hillside close to the Helvellyn track.

If you do both of the routes in Brown Cove, it is best to scramble Stepped Ridge (Route 75) first, descend the path and traverse into the combe again. Helvellyn is close and a walk along the ridge makes a splendid continuation.

77. Birkside Gill

Grade 2 ❋ *NY327125* 🏃🏃

Travellers over Dunmail Raise cannot fail to notice the attractive waterfalls in a gill close to the edge of the forest on the Thirlmere side of the pass. This is Birkside Gill, which cuts a valley into the broad back of Nethermost and Dollywaggon Pikes. This scramble, with its succession of clear green pools and cascades in a slight ravine, is ideal for a spare hour on a sunny afternoon.

Approach: Limited parking on the grass verge of the southbound carriageway on top of Dunmail Raise close to Raise Beck. Cross a stile and take a permissive path, left, signed 'Thirlmere'. This crosses a bridge on Raise Beck and leads just above the intake wall in ½ mile to a footbridge over Birkside Gill.

Route: Enter a small ravine below the footbridge to traverse a deep pool and climb a slab on the right. Another pool

Continuously interesting scrambling on solid, rough rock more akin to Langdale than Helvellyn makes this an attractive, if short scramble. Feasible only in dry conditions. Height gain 120m.

Birkside Gill has some good rock pitches

is crossed above the bridge to reach a cascade. Continue to a steeper fall, climbed on the left, and two more small cascades. After an easing of angle there are more cascades, the first guarded by a deep pool. Enter from the left and continue in the streambed to a more formidable fall, its narrow channel impassable unless dried up. Avoid it, left, and regain the stream above.

A broad rocky trough leads to a small steep fall whose mossy rocks are best avoided. Clean rocks on the left of a succession of small cascades lead to a narrow pool. Keep on the rocks, right, just above the water to gain a slabby trough ascended by straddling. Ahead is yet another deep pool backed by a striking cascade separated by a central rib from an overflow channel which provides a dry but sporting route. Move right near the top to finish up the central rib. This is the most serious pitch, but good holds appear when most needed. The angle relents as the stream cuts back into the hillside. A slight path descends the hillside diagonally back to the road.

BLENCATHRA (SADDLEBACK)

The southern and eastern slopes of this shapely mountain are sculpted into deep V-cut ravines, with smooth bilberry and heather flanks rising to slim rocky crests and a gently rounded summit slope. Nestling in a rocky combe is Scales Tarn, with the renowned Sharp Edge forming a sheltering arm to its north. The mountain is composed of Skiddaw Slate, which is sometimes unreliable, often smooth and slippery, and hence not as attractive for scrambling as it might be. Nevertheless, the rock on the ridge crests is safe and solid, well trodden by countless feet. The most attractive routes are time-honoured classics, two of the really good, albeit short, ridge scrambles in Lakeland – Sharp Edge and Hall's Fell Ridge. Both are best ascended, as the scrambling is less obvious on a descent when the easy option path is difficult to avoid.

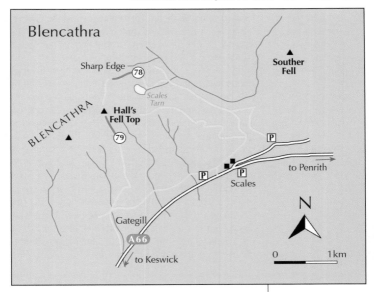

78. Sharp Edge

Grade 1✱✱✱ *NY328283*

Lakeland's sharpest ridge is justly popular. When the weather is kind the ascent is most enjoyable, leaving the scrambler with the wish that it continued in the same vein for much longer. It is one of the favourite introductory scrambles.

Approach: 400m along, on the Threlkeld side of Scales on the A66, are several laybys near the start of a path to the open fell. The track rises diagonally. At the first bend leave it for a lesser track straight ahead, which climbs then traverses to the head of Mousthwaite combe. (An alternative start is to park along the small lane at the foot of the combe and follow old mine tracks to its head.) An almost

197

It can be slippery when wet, a major undertaking in strong wind, and it is featured as a winter climb in the guide books, which should warn the walker or scrambler to keep away when there is snow on the ridge. About 150m height gain.

Sharp Edge and Scales Tarn

level track traverses the side of the Glenderamackin valley to reach the stream which issues from Scales Tarn. Ascend to the tarn, where a rounded grassy spur is climbed to the start of the ridge.

Route: Where the grass spur meets the first rocks do not take the walkers' path onto the north flank, but mount a rock groove onto the crest of the ridge. A well-scratched way is followed up the rocky ridge, with increasing exposure, along slabs, turrets and roof-like ridges where the choice is sometimes between a confident balancing act or a safety-first sit-shuffle. The crossing of a gap is the most awkward step, in an exposed position. The way is obvious and ends all too soon at a small col where the sharp horizontal ridge abuts the summit slopes. The easiest way to the summit is a trench-like groove which lies about 10m to the right in an exposed situation. This is steep at first then eases into a path which curls round the rim of the combe to the summit.

Descent of Sharp Edge

To reach the top of Sharp Edge from the summit follow a path northwards curling around the rim of the combe enclosing Scales Tarn and descend steepening slopes into a zone of shelving slabs. Aim for a groove with a steep right wall and follow this, encountering one steep step near its foot. This is all very exposed and becomes dangerous if slippery or if there is any snow about. Move right to reach a col at the head of the sharp arête where the ridge can be followed for the best scrambling. If it is windy it is wiser to take the walkers' path which runs below the crest, but even this requires care in bad conditions.

79. Hall's Fell Ridge

*Grade 1*** *NY326272*

The scramble involves a steep walk up a broad lower buttress, followed by pleasant rock scrambling along the crest of a sharp ridge. There is a soft-option walkers' path which is never far away.

This is a much easier and less exposed scramble than Sharp Edge, and the rock needs to be sought for maximum scrambling. Height gain 110m.

Approach: Park near Scales on the A66 (as for Sharp Edge, Route 78) and follow the track onto the open fell. Above the intake wall turn left where a track traverses the hillside across Scaley and Doddick becks to the base of a broad ridge, where a path is joined above Gategill. This point may be reached more directly from Threlkeld.

Route: The steep ascent of the initial slopes is repaid when the rock ridge is reached. There are no route-finding problems – just keep as close to the crest as possible (quite sharp in some places) and it emerges at the summit.

The combination of the two ridges makes a good, though short day. If you traverse the fell top to the south-west a return can be made at the base of the gills back to Scales.

PATTERDALE

Patterdale, with its many side-valleys, encompasses an extensive area which includes many fine rocky fells. Long approach valleys bite deep into the high fells of Helvellyn, Fairfield and High Street. There are excellent scrambles in gills and crags, which provide satisfying ways onto the higher fells. Pinnacle Ridge of St Sunday Crag is one the most popular routes in the Lakes. The rock is often smoother than that of other parts of the Lake District, and is slippery if damp, so care is needed. The scrambles are described in an anti-clockwise direction from Glenridding, incorporating all the side-valleys. There are campsites at Sykeside near Brothers Water, Side Farm near Patterdale, Glenridding, and many around the lower end of Ullswater.

Car parking and transport

Patterdale is very popular and the key car parking soon fills. There is a large car park at Glenridding, and smaller car parks at Patterdale, Brothers Water and Hartsop. Roadside parking is used in various places.

A bus service between Windermere and Glenridding runs daily in summer, but infrequently at other times.

HELVELLYN

The whole eastern side of Helvellyn and its satellite tops is gouged into deep rocky coves – a playground for winter climbers but a disappointment to the scrambler as the rock buttresses of the steep headwalls are discontinuous and vegetated. The scenery is first class. One of the most popular ridge walks is the circuit of Striding Edge and Swirral Edge, with some mild scrambling on the former. There are a few minor gill scrambles in Glenridding and a useful route to the tops on Eagle Crag Grisedale.

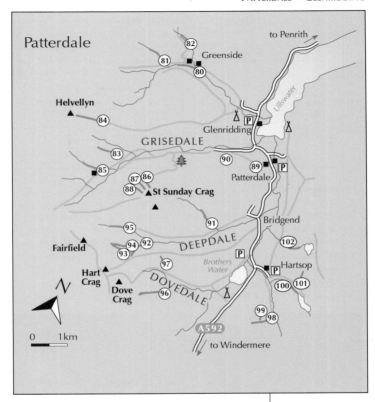

GLENRIDDING

A huge car park betrays the popularity of Glenridding as a lakeside tourist venue and the starting point for walks on Helvellyn. The valley was once a busy centre of the lead mining industry, and many of the old mine buildings at Greenside are now used by outdoor centres. The following short scrambles can be combined to make an interesting day.

Approach: Either use the large parking at Glenridding or drive a little further up the narrow valley road, where traffic is barred, to park just before a row of cottages. In winter cars are allowed as far as the mines, but the scrambles will often carry too much water at that time of year. Walk up the mines road to Greenside.

80. Greenside Ravine

Grade 1 ✳ NY337173 🔺

Entertaining traverses on attractively water-sculpted rock are features of the trip. The main fall is impossible and is avoided. Height gain 50m.

The main stream runs in a deep ravine just below the collection of houses. There is a particularly attractive waterfall, better than many more famous, but the only way to see it fully is from the bed of the ravine. The stream normally carries a strong flow which renders the expedition impossible; thus it is only practicable in a dry spell.

Approach: Gain the stream just before the houses.

In the Greenside Ravine

Route: Scramble on whichever rock bank offers a way to reach the first fall, passed easily on its left. The deeper gorge ahead is worth penetrating by a sporting ramp. This undulates along the right wall to reach the lip of a deep pool, into which drops a 20m waterfall –one of the most hidden in the Lakes. Unfortunately the pool and steep base of the fall are impassable; it is the sort of place the French would fix a wire *fil de fer* to facilitate passage, but here it is unthinkable, of course. Retrace steps along the ramp to broken ground and escape to the road. Just past a manhole cover you can regain the stream at the head of the fall. Traverse behind a tree and step down to gain a water-scoured alcove. Climb out of this to a rib. Follow the attractive rock bed, with a difficult stride over a deep inlet. Cross to the left to climb steep rocks to a weir. Final rocks are climbed under a bridge.

The next scramble lies up the small stream which pours over the lip of the craggy juniper-clad hillside on the right, a little further up the valley.

81. Rowten Beck

Grade 2✲ NY358172 🏔 ⚒

Approach: Follow the path up the right side of the valley to a footbridge over the stream. Walk up to where it becomes scrambly at the right branch below slabs.

Scrappy at first, it improves as height is gained. Height gain 120m.

Route: Pass through a jungle of small juniper. Climb slabs, move into the stream then up a belt of water-worn slabs. The main watercourse lies to the left and is best joined here to ascend a cascade. Continue in a slight defile. At a sharp bend the main scramble is revealed – three steep cascades topped by several minor steps. The first is 18m, steep and mossy; the second a low barrier climbed on the right. The third is another steep barrier which is best on the left. Interest is maintained in the smaller cascades above.

The trip finishes on the edge of an escarpment with the option of continuing to the tops at Raise or descending to reach Route 82. Follow the escarpment back towards Greenside to join the path which comes from the hamlet to the upper mines before the deep-cut stream. Turn down the path to a cairn and take a small path left along a terrace to mine dereliction. Where the terrace ends, the stream is easily gained.

82. Swart Beck (Sticks Gill)

Grade 3 ✳ *NY363178*

A short but interesting scramble up a steep-sided forbidding ravine. Only possible in low water. **A short rope and a long sling prove useful**. Height gain 30m.

Approach: As described after Route 81 from the top of Rowten Gill or by the Sticks Pass path from Greenside, which zigzags up the steep hillside above old spoil heaps. The track crosses scree and at a cairn turns steeply uphill. Continue past the cairn along a horizontal terrace through mine dereliction above the stream. You can see where a long-gone bridge crossed the ravine to the continuation of the terrace. At the end descend into the ravine,

Route: Pass a timber weir on its right to gain the narrower upper part of the ravine. Climb a steep rib on the right wall for 4m to a sapling, then move left to easier ground. The next hazard is a deep pool with a delicate traverse across a steep wall. Climb to a platform. The waterfall ahead blocks the ravine, but an escape can be made up the vertical left wall which has a series of good holds, the last of which proves to be shelving. It is easy to flick a sling over the spike above, which safeguards the move or can be used for aid. Cross the stream to finish on the right.

GRISEDALE

This long valley separates the Helvellyn range from that of Fairfield and is hugely popular as a gateway to the fells; for the walker on Striding Edge, Fairfield and St Sunday Crag; for the winter climber in the coves of Helvellyn; or for the visitor out on a stroll. There is little to suit the modern rock climber here, but high on the slopes of St Sunday Crag is a wealth of easy-angled good quality rock which gives fine scrambling. Whilst St Sunday Crag is the main attraction the other scrambles have their good points. Car parking at the valley entrance is very limited and it is better to use car parks at Patterdale or Glenridding.

83. Eagle Crag, Grisedale

Grade 2✱ NY356142

The rocks of Eagle Crag are a prominent feature on the walk up Grisedale, with old mine spoil heads at its foot.

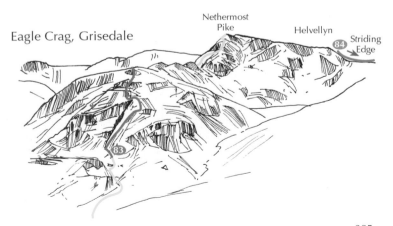

Eagle Crag, Grisedale

Nethermost Pike

Helvellyn

Striding Edge

The rocks give a scramble of over 150m, with a predominance of large flaky holds and spikes, **some of which need to be treated with caution**. Grass ledges are numerous and escape easy.

Approach: No cars are allowed to park up Grisedale, and the limited parking at the start of the valley lane by Grisedale Bridge soon fills. The large car park at Glenridding is useful if you combine the scramble with a walk on Helvellyn. A path over a low col at Lanty's Tarn contours into Grisedale. Another approach is from the car parking opposite the Patterdale Hotel, where a path traverses the slopes of Glenamara Park to drop into Grisedale at Thornhow. A good track then ensues up the valley past Elmhow to a branch right over a footbridge to gain the crags. Splitting the centre is a straight-cut gash of a mineral vein. On the right edge of this are the stepped

The delicate traverse to reach the flake on Eagle Crag, Grisedale

Eagle Crag detail

mine
spoil
heaps

ruin

slabs which form the basis of the route. Walk steeply up the right side of the mine spoil to a ruin. Go diagonally left below the first low rocks to the top of the scree cone.

Route: Start a few metres right of the gully vein. Ascend a smooth slabby nose then bear left to the foot of rocks at the gully edge. Keep close to the edge on good rock. At the level of a rowan is a prominent flake. Gain the foot of this by a delicate-to-start, leftward-rising ascent (avoidable on the left), then climb the right side of the flake. A shelf leads onto the front of the rib on the right to reach a grass terrace below a steep wall. From the cluster of flakes at its foot swarm straight up a steep flake, then move left over slabs to flakes on the edge. From the top of a pinnacle step right, behind a small tree, then up a leftward-slanting groove to a shelf with a knobbly edge on its left. Mount the knobbles to easy ground. Cross the top of the gully on the left to climb very smooth but gentle slabs above. Go left at the top and continue up a leaning block to a terrace. Pass a steep wall on its right to another terrace with an awkward exit up a slanting groove, which is steep at first. A short rock band ends the scramble.

Continuing up the broad spur leads to the rocky east ridge of Nethermost Pike, which makes a logical way onto the fell top. The ridge, which looks quite impressive in its upper part, proves to be a rough walk. Once on the top Helvellyn beckons, and Striding Edge provides a fine way back to Glenridding.

84. Striding Edge

Barely Grade 1✳✳✳ NY352150

Straightforward walking along the airy rocky ridge, which varies from a few feet wide to narrow with pinnacles.

The most popular ridge walk in the Lake District barely reaches the scrambling grade of this book, but is an experience savoured by every lover of Lakeland.

Approach: Park at Glenridding and reach the start of the ridge by the path over either Birkhouse Moor or Red Tarn. Cross a stile in the wall at the start of the ridge.

Route: Ignore the path on the northern flank and keep as much to crest to enjoy a flavour of scrambling. The only problem is the descent of a steep groove near the end of the ridge before it merges into the parent mountain.

Swirral Edge, the other bounding ridge of Red Tarn, is an exposed walk and makes a fine continuation after Striding Edge.

Grisedale has an unsatisfactory gill scramble up **Nethermost Beck**, which is composed of smooth slippery slabs, and a better gill scramble (Route 85) further up the valley.

Grisedale Beck below Eagle Crag runs in a slight ravine, which has an interesting scramble exit.

85. Ruthwaite Beck

Grade 2 ✳ *NY355136* ⚠

Approach: As for Eagle Crag (Route 83) then continue up the valley path on the right of the stream to the old stone cabin of Ruthwaite Lodge.

Route: A track leads into the gill from the hut and to an old mine level at the base of a cascade in a narrow ravine. The ascent of the left wall is the crux of the trip. The stream cascades over the right wall, which is too steep to climb, so exit on the right by a ledge, with a short descent at first. Regain the stream, now slabby. Climb the right wall of a small defile and exit with aid of a jutting tree. Slabs and a series of steps lead to another defile, climbed on the left to an awkward narrow trough. Start the final steep barrier by a slab on the right, and cross the spray-lashed ledge to finish on the left.

A short interesting ravine, slippery when wet but with good holds. Keep to the dry bits. Height gain 80m.

ST SUNDAY CRAG

High on the north-west slopes of St Sunday Crag a long line of crags overlooks Grisedale. The battlement of buttresses of rough rock is set at an angle ideal for scrambling. The rock stratum is also kind, for incuts and spiky holds abound. Pinnacle Ridge is one of Lakeland's classic scrambles – on everyone's tick-list. Haskett-Smith (1894) noted that the crags were long a favourite scrambling ground of Major Cundill. Nothing was recorded until the Sheffield University climbers based on nearby Ruthwaite Lodge explored the crags in the mid-1950s. Pinnacle Ridge is the crowded classic, but the other more difficult scrambles have a quieter mountaineering atmosphere.

86. Pinnacle Ridge

Grade 3✱✱✱ NY368138

Slabs, blocks and a steep, sometimes greasy crux to enjoy. Some of the blocks may be unstable, so care is needed. Avoid if windy. Escape paths exist around all the difficult sections. **Rope advised** for the short crux. Height gain 150m.

The much photographed alpine-type sharp ridge is just one short stretch of this varied trip.

Approach: The simplest approach is from Grisedale Bridge, but the parking soon fills. Alternatively park at Patterdale, where a path from the back of the Patterdale Hotel traverses Glenamara Park to drop into Grisedale at a sheepfold. Walk up the valley track until just past Elmhow. Branch left at the far side of a plantation and go left at its top. Above find the Elmhow Zigzags, indeterminate at first, then a smooth grassy path which gains height easily up the steep hillside to a grassy shelf at Blind Cove. Fork right on a small path across an almost level shelf. Where it runs into steeper hillside ascend a little to a small reedy hollow. Keep left round this and up to a small but useful traversing path across the steep hillside. Cross two small scree shoots then a larger one which runs the

St Sunday Crag

Pinnacle Ridge · Broad Buttress · cairn · 86 · 87 · East Chockstone Gully · tiger-banded rocks · from Elmhow Zigzags · scree · path

The final pinnacles of Pinnacle Ridge

full length to the crags at the foot of Pinnacle Ridge. Ascend the side of the scree to the base of the ridge, which is an easy-angled jumble of blocks and boulders. There is a rowan about 45m up the right-hand side. A prominent gun-like block higher up the ridge is another landmark.

Route: Start at a small cairn on the left of a gully and scramble up spiky blocks on the edge of the buttress. There is a very good stretch of scrambling on an exposed edge overlooking the gully below the gun-like block. The gun is supported by a slabby prow. Mount a few feet up this and avoid its final smooth slab by bearing right behind the back of a block. The broken ridge continues to the base of a large pinnacle, avoided on the left. At the back of this is a short steep wall, the crux. There is a thread belay block in the back of the often greasy groove. Climb the groove on good holds, exit left, then move right onto the crest to another steepening. Avoid this by a stepped slab on the left and belay on the spiky crest of the ridge. The exposed pinnacled crest is traversed to where it abuts against a slab. Pull left over the sharp top and descend an exposed slab to a neck. Scramble easily up the other side to bilberry slopes. Bear left to finish up a staircase of blocks through quite steep rock.

A ridge walk over Fairfield followed by a return by the southern rim of Deepdale, or an easier return by Grisedale, makes a good day.

Other scrambles exist on the jumble of St Sunday Crag, but they have to conquer a band of steep rock to access the more amenable terrain above. Two are described below.

87. Broad Buttress, St Sunday Crag
Grade 3✹✹ *NY367138*

This is the wide buttress between Pinnacle Ridge and East Chockstone Gully.

Approach: From the foot of Pinnacle Ridge walk to the right-hand corner of the buttress close to the gully.

Route: At the right end of the buttress between the bounding rib of the steep smooth slabs and the gully is a lesser-angled light-coloured rib in the middle of a recess. Cairn. Climb the rib and slab on the left of a corner to a grass shelf. Go left a metre or so to the foot of a pale grey slabby rib with a perched block at its base. Climb the rib for 2m then ease behind the block. Cross a steep wall to a rock ledge on the left. Continue up and left to a bilberry groove. Go up to the base of this and traverse 10m left to a clean rib. Climb this and continue the traverse to easy ground. Ascend a short mossy wall to ledges. This completes the leftwards tour to avoid the steep band of dark grey, rather vegetated, rock.

Return to the right edge of the buttress by a walk, right, along a bilberry shelf. Climb broken rocks just left of the edge to a groove. Climb a rib on the left to broken ground. Bear right towards the edge overlooking the gully. A steeper crag looms above. Climb broken rocks about 15m left of the edge and slant diagonally right into a recess with a huge perched block. Climb carefully between blocks to a rib of good rock to a bilberry platform. Ascend diagonally left towards a chimney, then diagonally right up into a groove. Climb this by the side of a block and exit on its top right. An exposed staircase on the edge of the gully leads to a boulder-strewn terrace.

The steep wall above presents several choices. One of the best ways is a rib rising from square blocks just left of a slabby recess. Climb across a slab to reach the block

A devious and intricate route with some loose blocks. Exposure is considerable and **a rope is advised**. The lower band of steep dark grey rock is unsuitable for scrambling, and the route seeks an easier way round this. Two steep areas of crag above succumb remarkably easily. Height gain 150m.

and mount a 3m crack to a flat-topped pedestal. A steep step above brings good holds and easy slopes.

For the competent seeking further scrambling, a **descent of Pinnacle Ridge** is feasible. On the left across the top of a gully is the obvious crest of well-used rock. Sheep tracks lead across the gully screes to the top of the ridge. Descent is straightforward, although care is necessary. It is not easy to judge the stability of some of the numerous flakes from above. For most enjoyment, seek out the true rock scramble which more or less follows the crest. The descent of the steep groove into the gap behind the pinnacle is easier than it appears.

88. South-West Buttress, St Sunday Crag

Grade 4 NY365135*

The first pitch is the hardest and needs a steady leader. **Rope advised.** Height gain 150m.

Another rambling route based on the crags either side of West Chockstone Gully, which more or less bounds the crags on the right. This serious scramble with a mountaineering atmosphere seeks the best way on either side of the gully.

Approach: From the base of Pinnacle Ridge, follow the small path right below the crags. The first deep gully is East Chockstone Gully. To the right of this is a broad buttress with the 'tiger-banded rocks' at its foot. Continue the traverse past Pillar Gully and the very deep Y-Gully which hosts the best rock climbs on a steep crag at its back. West Chockstone Gully marks the end of the horizontal path, and the following route starts up the slabby rib on its left.

Route: The rib is easy at first, but holds become sparse where the rock type changes. Keep left of the edge, and holds appear where needed. Step back right and finish up the edge to a bilberry terrace and belay below an impending wall. Cross a ledge on the right wall of the gully to a grass ledge which leads into a smaller gully round the corner. Climb the slabby bed, move left onto slabs and avoid a bedded stone in the corner. The edge of the rib above is climbed airily, overlooking the gully. At its top is an easy crossing of the gully to gain more attractive rocks on its left. Cross the gully, descending slightly to gain slabs on the far side. Climb these for 9m to a ledge, left, onto the buttress front. Walk left along a flat narrow ledge to climb a rib below a jutting block. Below the block move right and ascend to a terrace. Climb a rib on the left to emerge on a bilberry hillside.

The following two very short scrambles make an aperitif to the routes on Eagle Crag or St Sunday Crag. They are both used as an introduction to climbing for youngsters.

89. Oxford Crag

Grade 2 NY393154

Here you can judge if you are happy to climb unroped before tackling more serious fare.

Approach: Park at Patterdale and go behind the hotel to a path which traverses into the shallow valley of Glenamara Park. From a gate, the crag is reached in a few minutes' steep walk by the wall. It is well worn at its base.

Route: You can climb virtually anywhere, but it is steeper, more interesting and at its highest in the middle.

A steep short crag covered in holds – it makes a good introduction. Height gain 15m.

90. Grisedale Slabs, Thornhow Crag

Grade 2✻ NY382154

A taste of scrambling, with good positive fingergrips, makes this short route worth a diversion. Height gain 20m.

Approach: As for Oxford Crag (Route 89) but continue on the main path through the gate, across Glenamara Park and contour through light woods into Grisedale. Through a gate descend slightly to a sheepfold, where the main path descends to the valley track. From the sheepfold walk a little further along the path above the wall. A steep crag is obvious ahead. Your route lies on the left-hand crag at a higher level.

Route: At the right end of the left-hand crag, set at a higher level, is a clean slab. Start below the right end of an overhung shelf and climb the right edge of a short slab.

Grisedale slabs are short but pleasant.
Photo: G.Dewitt

Grisedale Slabs

climbing crag

path

Move left along the ledge, up onto a flake on the right. The slab steepens at the top to an abrupt finish.

DEEPDALE

The long bare valley of Deepdale, with Fairfield at its head, is reminiscent of a Scottish glen. Approach is from Bridgend, 1 mile south of Patterdale village. There is limited roadside parking by the telephone box at Bridgend and other car parking at either Cow Bridge to the south or Patterdale village.

91. Coldcove Gill

Grade 1 NY391136*

The stream which drains the eastern side of St Sunday Crag makes its final descent into Deepdale over a very rocky bed.

Approach: Park by the telephone kiosk at Bridgend. Take a rough lane to Lanehead, where the path up Deepdale goes left. Just past Wallend farm reach the open fell, and your gill is the first stream of any consequence.

Pleasant, very easy scrambling often on broad slabs which, if dry, could be walked. Not serious – a good outing for novices on excellent rock. Height gain 90m.

Route: Start at a holly a short way above the valley path. Broad slabs lead to a slight ravine. Go up the waterchute close to the steep right wall. The ravine narrows, and a short steep fall at its head is passed by a crawl along an overhung ledge on the right. Walk to another belt of slabs guarded by a short pool. Cross the right side of this to gain slabs, which are climbed up a slippery chute on the right. More walking leads to a final narrowing and an abrupt exit.

Gavel Pike, the shapely outlier of St Sunday Crag, is ahead, or the scrambles on St Sunday Crag (Routes 86–88) could be reached by crossing a col between it and Birks. Alternatively, return to the valley by a path through the bracken on the south side of the stream and continue to the scrambles further up Deepdale.

92. Link Cove Gill

Grade 2 or 3✳✳✳ *NY375122* 🔺 ⛏⛏

This is the stream which descends from Link Cove into Deepdale. Good rock and interesting pitches of great

Link Cove Gill

Greenhow End

Link Cove

Cofa Pike

Sleet Cove

variety and beauty make this a splendid expedition in one of Lakeland's most entertaining gills. Combined with the scramble on Greenhow End it makes a fine route onto Fairfield.

Approach: From Bridgend follow the track up Deepdale for 3½km. The main track begins to rise away from the stream, so take a smaller path threading through an area of drumlins, directly towards the side-stream issuing from Link Cove on the left.

Route: The first scrambling is at a slabby cascade, and makes a good introduction to the rough knobbly rock. Keep to the left-hand branch on pleasant slabs into a narrow ravine. Traverse the left wall of a shallow pool and climb the cascade. The next obstacle is similar but more fearsome (perhaps passable in drought), so escape to the slabs above the right edge of the ravine. (These slabs provide a viable grade 2 alternative.) An exposed way at the top of the fall drops back into the gill and yet another pool with its attendant cascade. Traverse the pool on its left and either climb the cascade cleft damply or take a dry groove on its left.

Emerge into a fine slabby amphitheatre, steepening at the top, which provides the crux passage of the direct route with a pitch of v diff rock climbing. Zigzag easily up the first half. A belay is advisable before the exposed finish. Climb a fine slab just left of the cascade, but you will be forced into the edge of the flow at the finish. From the halfway point an escape can be made, left, to an exposed finish below a tree. A rope slung over the tree will provide protection. An easier alternative climbs the slabs on the right of the ravine. A variety of entertaining ways can be taken up the next cascades, the ravine merging into open hillside.

Follow the streambed to a sharp left-hand bend before striking rightwards to the rocks of Greenhow End (Routes 93 and 94), which provide the logical continuation and a fine way to the summit of Fairfield.

Best tackled in a dry spell – too much water necessitates bypassing some of the best parts. Be prepared to get damp. **Rope is needed** for a crucial pitch which needs an **experienced leader**. Height gain 120m.

93. The Light Slabs, Greenhow End

Grade 1 or 2✷✷ *NY371120*

Open scrambling of a pleasant nature on rough rock. Height gain 120m.

This is the rocky termination of the ridge which extends from Fairfield and separates Link Cove and Sleet Cove at the head of Deepdale.

Approach: After scrambling up Link Cove Gill the slabs are on the right. There is a grass rake which zigzags

Greenhow End

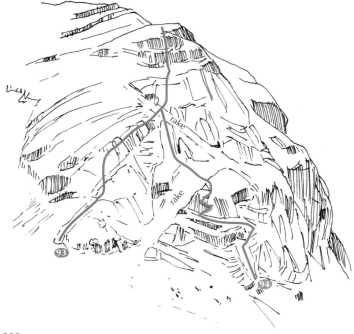

up; the scramble takes the light-coloured slabs to the left of this.

Route: About 10m left of a small tree follow the cleanest rocks. Bear right to gain the clean pale slabs. Easy continuous scrambling, searching for the best rock, ends at a platform close to the easy cairned grass rake. Cross to the rock rib on the right. Scramble pleasantly to another large terrace on the zigzag rake. Cross this and ascend the steep wall opposite a cairn, just left of a nose. Zigzag left then back right on a ledge with a strenuous pull up a steep corner, which can be avoided further left. A knobbly rib ends the good scrambling, although several rocky steps are encountered along the ridge towards Fairfield.

94. The Dark Slabs, Greenhow End

*Grade 2 or 3**✱✱** NY371120*

Approach: As for Route 93, but this takes the initial rocks right of the grassy rake.

Route: Start up a paler slabby rib which descends from a steep upper wall. Climb the rib to below the steep wall, where a flanking traverse is required via two grass ledges diagonally rightwards, then back left to gain a grass terrace above the nasty bit. The wall above looks forbidding, so walk left along the terrace under a clean slab. If you do not like the look of this slab, walk on and escape, but it proves easier than it appears and provides a fine grade 3 pitch (**rope advised**). Climb a right-slanting groove for 6m, move horizontally left on good footledges for 6m, then take a rightward-slanting line to finish under a prominent jutting block.

Scramble up clean slabs on the right to gain the terrace at the top of the grassy rake. You now take the slabs which bound the walkers' continuation gully on its left. First climb on the left of a slippery corner, then go up

A more difficult way up the slabs, more interesting than Route 93 and more in keeping with the standard of scrambling in Link Cove Gill (Route 92), if you have done the hard way. Height gain 120m.

open slabs which terminate near the top of the gully at a junction with Route 93. Cross to a rocky rib on the right and go up to cross another terrace. Easy rock steps complete the route.

The ridge provides some rock interest on the way to Fairfield. Note that there is no safe descent into Deepdale until the large scree shoots well past Hutable Crag. It is preferable to complete the day with a traverse of Hart Crag and the Hartsop above How Ridge which forms the southern boundary of Deepdale. It is possible to descend a short way from this to reach the scramble on Gill Crag (Route 97).

95. Deepdale Beck

Grade 2 ✳ *NY371125* 🔺

Not serious, but some ability is required to solve the various rock traverses above deep pools. Any difficulties can be avoided by an excursion out of the ravine, but this diminishes the fun. Good rock. Height gain 40m.

When walking up the valley the straight-cut cleft of Link Cove Gill is mirrored by a similar cleft to the right where the main stream drops into the broad drumlin-filled hollow of Mossydale. This cleft provides the scramble.

Approach: Walk up Deepdale from Bridgend to the enchanting hollow of drumlins below the steep cone of Greenhow End. At the entrance of the rocky cleft, the main path rises steeply on the right.

Route: Climb slabs to enter the small ravine, which soon shows its character when the first deep pool is reached. Traverse the steep left wall on good holds. Pass the next pool on the right slabs and another direct. It becomes easier, but good sport is found close to the stream. At another pool, cross a ledge on the left wall, then cross the stream and ascend direct. You are faced with a long deep pool with steep side-walls. It is easy to escape left and regain the streambed above, but it is possible to cross the steep left wall, which involves a bold swing round a prow above the deepest part of the pool. Ahead is another narrow pool – not quite so ferocious, but still quite intimidating. Start on the left wall then straddle the deep water and shuffle into the safety of its narrows. Easier rock on the left of the stream emerges in the upper drumlin hollow of Sleet Cove, below Hutable Crag.

DOVEDALE

This steep, short valley which joins Patterdale near Brothers Water has the impressive Dove Crag at its head.

96. Hogget Gill

Grade 1 or 3 ✳ NY387109 🔺 🌿🌿

Approach: There is a car park at Cow Bridge just below Brothers Water. A lakeside path runs up the valley to Hartsop Hall. Alternatively, park on the A592 near the

Hoggett Gill

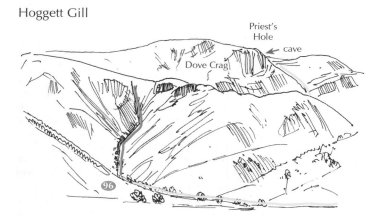

An interesting easy ascent if the water-course is followed closely. Difficulties can be avoided. The rock is often slippery, and care is needed with loose flakes. The direct grade 3 pitch is worth doing. Height gain 250m.

Brothers Water Inn and walk through Sykes Farm campsite to Hartsop Hall. Keep straight on the lower path into the flat valley floor to cross a footbridge over Dovedale Beck. Bear left into the valley of Hogget Gill to enter a wooded ravine.

Route: Walking through the wooded ravine brings the first waterfall into view. This is difficult to ascend direct except in drought, but an interesting solution is to start up rocks on the right flank, cross the stream at half-height and gain a grass terrace on the left wall. Do not go up the tempting groove, but walk left to reach an easier tree-filled groove. This fall can be avoided. Pleasant scrambling above goes past a steep fall by a loose corner to a delightful stretch where the stream runs in a V-trench with a slabby right wall. Keep on the slabs close to the watercourse.

The grade 3 variant pitch in Hogget Gill.
Photo: M.Tedd

The gill changes character and becomes floored with a jumble of boulders. Thread a way through and over these to a waterfall. The **grade 1** way requires a short detour out of the gill by the grassy left wall to regain the stream above the obstacle. A **grade 3** pitch ascends this by a rising traverse of the left wall rightwards to the top of the fall. The traverse is awkward to start but becomes easier after the first couple of moves.

Take the left-hand stream at a confluence, and for the most sporting finish cross the grassy shoulder to regain the right-hand stream.

Exit on the fell with the summit of Little Hart Crag close by. An interesting walk is to traverse the slopes on the right to gain the combe below Dove Crag, scene of some of Lakeland's fiercest rock climbs. There is no scrambling here, but a dark slit, the **Priest's Hole**, high on the right side of the crag can be reached by a path further right. It is a wide low slot approached by a rising traverse scramble.

97. Flake Buttress, Gill Crag

Grade 3✳✳ NY387119

This attractive crag with a sunny aspect is situated high on the northern flank of Dovedale. It hosts several rock climbs of a mild nature, and the easiest of these is adapted to make the following scramble.

Approach: From Cow Bridge parking near Brothers Water or from Sykeside reach Hartsop Hall. Take the upper fork just past the hall and skirt the lower edge of the wood. Go through a gate and make a very steep rough ascent close to the wall to reach the base of the slabs on the left.

It is also feasible to approach from above, on the Hartsop above How ridge. The wall is a key landmark,

Slabs with a multitude of holds are a feature of this route. Exposure is felt as height is gained, and although the climbing is straightforward **a rope is advised** for all but the most confident. Height gain 50m.

Gill Crag location

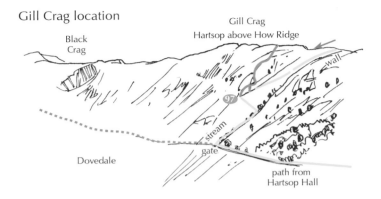

Black
Crag

Gill Crag
Hartsop above How Ridge

wall

97

stream

gate

Dovedale

path from
Hartsop Hall

and where it drops into a gully traverse below the top rocks, then rough ground gives access to the base of the crag.

Route: The easiest way up the lower tier is at the left-hand end. From the right edge of a boulder climb the mossy wall, moving left at the top to the long grass terrace of Birdcage Walk. Walk up the terrace to a corner behind

Gill Crag

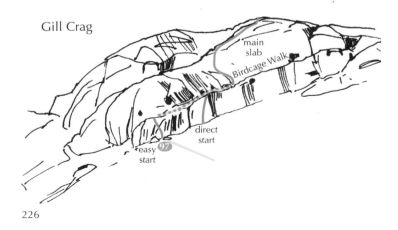

main
slab

Birdcage Walk

direct
start

easy
start

97

some yews. A flake forms the right wall of the corner. This point can be reached by a more difficult direct start. The slabs above are easier than they look. Climb easily up the right-hand side of the flake and continue on big holds to a grass ledge. Climb the slabs above, trending slightly left. Do not go into the grassy recess unless you want to belay, but mount the rib edge, back right, keeping just on the front face to make best use of holds. At its top, knobbly slabs on the left offer sport. A block gives a good finish by a crack on its left.

The bulk of this route is the left side of the **Main Slab**, the centre of which is a **v diff** climb on good small holds with no protection.

THRESHTHWAITE COVE

98. Central Route, Raven Crag
Grade 4✳ NY419113

This deep-cut side-valley lies to the east of the main Patterdale valley, which it joins at Hartsop. The most dominant feature is the steep dark Raven Crag on its right. This is very steep in its lower part, then lessens in angle and culminates in an interesting stepped ridge. **Access restrictions usually apply in the bird-nesting season.**

Approach: There is a car park at the top end of Hartsop village. Cross the stream and follow the path on the far side into the valley. A stone wall runs up the hillside to the base of the crag.

Route: Just above the wall, a broad grass terrace runs from left to right. Branching left from this are other terraces – the first leads into steep rock; you take the second. This rises leftwards in a series of steps, with most rock on its left edge. The terrace steepens into a vegetated gully.

The rock is a very sound volcanic ash characterized by rough knobbles which give a satisfying grip, yet it is inadvisable when wet. **There are some serious and exposed situations.** Intricate route finding in the lower half adds to the interest. Rope advised. Height gain 200m.

Avoid the first nasty bit of the gully by an excursion onto the slabs on the right. Circle back into the gully and climb it for about 18m until the rock rib on the left can be crossed to the easy-angled front of the buttress. This section is **steep and serious**, and the **correct choice of route is critical**.

Once on the broad front of the buttress the situation eases for a while, with pleasant scrambling to a grass ledge at the foot of a steepening. From the top left of this grass climb a rock gangway up right for 5m, then traverse horizontally right to the arête which has good holds and leads to easier ground.

A grass rake slants leftwards into a rocky bay, which provides a fitting climax to the serious scrambling and exits just below the crest of the ridge and a junction with Tower Route. Cross the steep rock wall opposite by a narrow terrace from left to right until slabs can be

Raven Crag, Threshthwaite Cove

Raven Crag, Threshthwaite Cove, detail

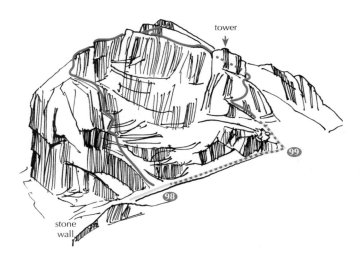

climbed. Walk to the next step in the ridge, which provides a sting in the tail. Surmount it by crossing a slab to the right of a prominent neb.

99. Tower Route, Raven Crag

Grade 2✻ NY419113

Approach: As for Route 98. **Access restrictions usually apply in the bird-nesting season.**

Route: Above the stone wall, follow the rising grass terrace from left to right for about 90m to a tree growing in the foot of a rock spur. Either scramble up the rocks of this spur or avoid them by another grass terrace on its

An easier scramble than Route 98, based on the buttress on the right of the main crag and left of a grass corridor. Escapable in most parts, it finishes up the stepped ridge of Route 98. Height gain 200m.

right. In either case, head for the foot of a clean rock rib. At the base of this rib, take a narrow gangway which slopes from right to left to a recess, where a traverse diagonally right brings an easing in angle to the foot of a fine tower. A direct ascent of this poses rock-climbing problems, so scramblers are advised to escape into the grass gully on its right. Above the tower, return to the crest of a rock rib on the left for pleasant easy progress to the ridge. There are two steps in the ridge – the first is crossed by a ledge from left to right; the second provides a fine climax with a short sharp ascent by a slab to the right of a prominent neb.

The slopes to the north of the crag provide an easy descent.

✳ ✳ ✳

100. Hayeswater Gill

Grade 1 or 2 ✳ NY423129

The scramble is mainly in a low-walled ravine with occasional steps. The rock is good, though slippery where wet. Nowhere serious, you can seek difficulties or avoid them. Best in a dry spell. Height gain 100m.

This is a most unlikely setting for a scramble as the valley seems hardly steep enough, yet parts are surprisingly good. The stream drains the eastern side of High Street, where a deep trench-like valley curls into the hills from Hartsop. Its ascent can enliven a walk to the tops – the scene is attractive, with several beautiful deep pools and water-worn cavities.

Approach: Go through the attractive village of Hartsop to a car park. Continue up the waterworks road up the north side of the main valley to a building where a path branches to the right across the river at a footbridge.

Route: From the footbridge follow the stream past two slab barriers to enter a rocky defile. The first pool presents a tricky obstacle. If dry enough, traverse the left

Scrambling Hayeswater Gill in winter

side to climb a steep little wall in the overflow channel. Otherwise detour out of the gill on the right. Another little defile soon follows. Traverse the steep left wall close to the water with good handholds. The 4m-wide ravine culminates in a circular pool backed by a cascade. In very dry conditions a direct route may be possible, but more usually an escape must be made up the left wall, close to the entrance of the pool, by a steep zigzag ascent around trees. The rock exit, on spiky holds, needs care. Note the side-stream **Sulphury Gill** which enters on the left, as this makes a pleasant continuation after finishing Hayeswater Gill. Walk a few metres up the main stream to another defile which contains a small cascade, climbed on either side.

Hayeswater is a short way up the valley along the broad track which has accompanied the gill on the right. However, if further scrambling is desired, traverse the hillside on the left descending slightly to gain Sulphury Gill.

101. Sulphury Gill

Grade 1 NY426128

There is plenty of choice on good staircase-like rock. Height gain 80m.

This is the side-stream already noted at the start of a long sweep of slabby rock.

Route: The right-hand channel is the most interesting. Several rock steps prolong the scramble to easier-angled slopes and join the path from Angle Tarn to High Street.

102. Angle Tarn Beck

Grade 1 or 2 NY406140

An open gill with some waterslides and cascades in its lower half. Only worth doing in dry conditions, as the rocky bed is narrow and completely filled in high water. Height gain 150m.

This stream flows down the steep eastern side of Patterdale, below Angletarn Pikes, and provides the only worthwhile scrambling approach to the tops in this area.

Approach: The car park at Hartsop is the best choice, as this allows a return over High Street. From the car park walk into the village and take the first lane on the right. This becomes a path that passes Eden Beck and descends through woods to the slightly larger Angle Tarn Beck.

Route: Do not miss the lowest cascades are these are scrambled on excellent rock. There is an easing of angle before a series of cascades that are as difficult as you care to make them. Above the woods the stream provides no further interest. More scrambling can be incorporated by taking to the buttress on the left at a bend in the stream by a large tree. This buttress has been well visible on the way up the stream and has a prominent perched capstone. There is a choice of ways on spiky rock. Care is required as there are quite a lot of unattached blocks, although the parent rock is quite good. Pleasant scrambling, past several small trees, in two rock steps leads to the top of the crags, then a walk to Angle Tarn.

The twin summits of nearby Angletarn Pikes are quite rocky, and the diligent scrambler will find more sport.

103. Swarthbeck Gill, Arthur's Pike

Grade 3 NY453207

On the steep slopes of Arthur's Pike, overlooking the lower third of Ullswater, is the deep ravine of Swarthbeck Gill.

Approach: Parking on the narrow lane below the gill is virtually impossible, so it is best to continue past Howtown, where there is parking when the road takes to open fell. Gain the line of an aqueduct at Mellguards near the Howtown Hotel and follow the bridleway to the base of the gill. A recommended alternative is to park at Pooley Bridge and take the lake steamer to Howtown. This allows a pleasant walk to finish along the gentle fell top.

Route: Enter the gill past large boulders and walk close to the stream to a double waterfall. The top one is climbed by a mossy scoop on its left, then escape left under a large boulder flake. A walk follows to the foot of the upper falls in a narrow enclosed ravine. Traverse the left side of the bottom pool of the upper section on sloping holds to the right, where a short but strenuous move leads to an insecure slab between the stream and the steep right wall. At the top of this pull up on doubtful holds and lurch across the streamway. Go up this a short way then onto the left bank near a birch tree. Above a higher birch regain the streamway below a short fall which marks the end of the scramble.

    Alternative finish (grade 4): Before entering the upper ravine there are easy escapes, but a determined

A vegetated ravine with some loose and slippery rock, advisable only in a very dry spell. **Access restrictions usually apply in the bird-nesting season.** Height gain 150m.

scrambler can force a route up the vegetated crags on the left wall by an exposed serious scramble. First follow a faint track on the left wall to an awkward rock step. The track continues to a slabby groove which gives good scrambling to exit on the side of the ravine.

There is a descent path on the right of the ravine, but a walk along the fell top is more attractive. The tall cairn of Bonscale Tower is quite close and is a fine viewpoint.

BOREDALE

The following gill scrambles, used by the nearby outdoor centre, lie at the head of the remote valley of Boredale. Both could also be approached over Boredale Hause from Patterdale.

Boredale Head Gill has nice rock and a sunny aspect

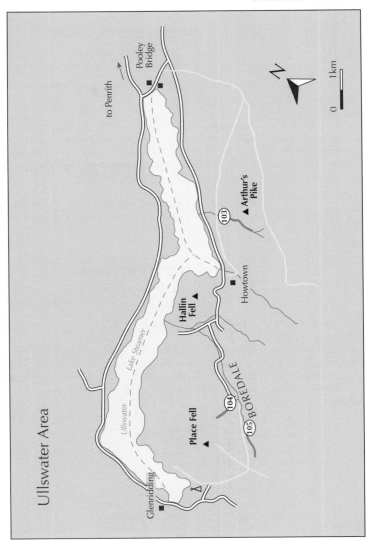

Ullswater Area

104. Boredale Head Gill

Grade 1✳ NY419171

The rock is slippery where wet, and for best sport this route needs low water. The stratum is favourable. Full ascent gives 260m height gain.

This is an open gill with a sunny aspect, which can be escaped anywhere.

Approach: A minor road runs along the south-east side of Ullswater from Pooley Bridge. At Howtown continue over the hairpin road towards Sandwick. Go straight on up Boredale to park at the road end. The gill is immediately above.

Route: Keep in the rock bed, which gives interesting scrambling for a long way, the lower half being the best.

105. Freeze Beck

Grade 2 NY413168 🌿

Only worth doing in low water, wearing socks to combat the very slippery rock. Escape is possible at numerous points. Height gain 120m.

A gloomy low slit-ravine.

Approach: As for Route 104, but from the parking walk up the bridleway to the valley head. Where the track rises, follow a small path above the wall and continue by the stream to enter the obvious ravine of Freeze Beck.

Route: The ravine is a succession of short falls, pools and narrows. There is a longer pitch near the top.

MARDALE

The head of Mardale is an interesting rocky place, yet the scrambling possibilities are limited. The most rewarding route lies in the impressive combe which encircles Blea Water, one of Lakeland's deepest ice-gouged tarns, where a steep back wall sweeps up to the gentle swell of the summit ridge of High Street. The northerly arm of the Blea Water combe is the upper part of Long Stile ridge, a justly popular walkers' way onto the High Street plateau from Mardale. Riggindale, on the other side of the Long Stile →

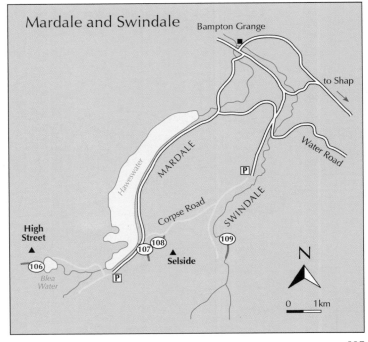

← ridge, is renowned as the nesting site for the Lake District eagles, which can often be seen soaring over the area. The only other good scrambling is found in the gills above Haweswater.

Car parking
There is a car park at the road end and numerous places along the roadside above Haweswater. The most popular spots soon fill at busy times.

106. Blea Water Crag Gill

Grade 3 ✱✱ *NY446106* 🏔 🌲🌲

The steep hillside encircling Blea Water is composed of numerous small crags, with a prominent central gully cutting deep into the upper crags. To the left of this gully is a less obvious watercourse which falls over a number

Blea Water Crag Gill

of slabby cascades to culminate in a short narrow cleft just above the lake. This varied scramble, based on the gill and its overflow channels, provides an interesting way to the summit plateau.

Approach: From the valley-head car park a path runs up the valley. Turn right almost immediately to cross the main stream and follow the path on the left. This climbs steadily to Blea Tarn, where a small traversing path on the right side of the lake peters out. Scramble along the rocky shore then mount to the base of the cleft.

Route: The first deep cleft is only feasible in dry conditions, when a damp ascent can be made. Climb up the back of the cleft, then escape left onto a half-way ledge, which can be gained more easily by avoiding the problem on the left. The upper part of the cleft has a difficult

The scrambling is unlike that in a true gill, and is often exposed, serious and difficult. **Rope advised**. Best climbed in dry conditions as the rock becomes very slippery when damp. Height gain 220m.

Don't go to Blea Water Crag Gill too early in the season, or you may find the first cleft full if ice!

239

exit and is more often avoided by a zigzag left to regain the gill above the difficulty. Walk round a black fall on its right and up a ramp above, about 10m past the next fall, where rocks lead back to the streambed to gain the base of a waterslide.

A direct ascent is impracticable, so walk a few metres left to a slabby recess. Slant from left to right up the easiest way. This is a subsidiary water channel with a tricky exit onto grass ledges. Descend slightly right to the main stream and the end of the most difficult scrambling. The line is now obvious for a considerable distance. Just keep to the main stream or its overflows, up a succession of cascades, until the stream lessens in angle near the top. Now transfer to the sharp little ridge on the right, which provides a fitting climax.

A gentle stroll to the summit of High Street can be followed by a descent of the Long Stile Ridge back to Mardale, thus combining the best scramble in the area with the finest ridge walk. A longer return can be made crossing the top of Nan Bield Pass and Harter Fell to the Gatescarth Pass where the old pony track descends to the car park.

107. Hopgill Beck

*Grade 2** NY481117*

It is only feasible in a dry spell. When the rocks are damp they are treacherously slippery and socks over footwear are advised. In a dry spell there are still a few slippery patches. Height gain 100m.

The main stream which cuts into Selside Pike is Rowantreethwaite Gill. Hopgill Beck is a less noticeable side-stream which runs in a narrow ravine. It offers continuously interesting scrambling – at first in a verdant ravine, then on open rocks. Both gills provide good sport, and if Hopgill Beck is climbed first the interesting upper part of Rowantreethwaite Gill is easily reached.

Approach: Follow the road alongside Haweswater until opposite the island near the head of the lake. A car may

*The entry pitch of Hopgill Beck
is climbed in socks*

be parked close to the bridge, or better up the hill 30m north near the start of the Old Corpse Road, which was used by the villagers of the now submerged Mardale to take their dead over to Shap before their own church was consecrated.

Route: From the road bridge go through a gate and up the main stream to where Hopgill Beck enters over a steep rock barrier on the right. Traverse the pool from the right and climb steep rocks on the right of the lip of the fall. The holds are good. Pass two small mossy falls on the left to reach a much steeper fall over a jammed block. Bypass this on the left and re-enter the gill. Cross a pool on boulders to pass the next spout. The gill bends right to exit from the shadowy ravine.

Ahead the stream runs over rocks which afford good scrambling on slabs left of the flow. At the top of the slabs cross below a steep wall into the stream on good flake-holds to gain a left-hand channel. A mossy fall guards the entrance to another ravine. Pass it on the right over steep boulders. A deep pool is bypassed to regain the damp rocks of the gill. Pass the next fall by a dry route on the right. The gill continues past another cascade on the right and, finally, slabs on the left to finish by a large tree.

Reach the interesting part of Rowantreethwite Gill by traversing the hillside. Descend a very steep grass slope to gain the bed of the gill.

108. Rowantreethwaite Gill

Grade 3 ✱✱ *NY480118*

Approach: As for Route 107.

Route: The stream drops in a series of cascades over the steep right-hand wall near the top of the main stony gill. Start on the right by a ramp round the back of a large

On the delicate, airy crux slab of
Rowantreethwaite Gill

The approach is barely more than a walk. The climax is a splendid serious pitch which requires low water and perhaps socks over footwear for a safe ascent. Comparable with the main pitch in Ashness Gill (Route 45) but easier. Height gain 60m.

sycamore. Alternatively, ascend more directly to the same ledge. From the ledge climb steep stepped rooty rock for 10m to another ledge. The steep slabby groove above, on the right of the fall, is the exposed tricky crux. The situation eases, and a dry overflow is climbed left of the main mossy fall. Pass the next cascade easily on its left and continue to meet a sheep track which crosses the gill where the scramble ends.

Follow the sheep track left across the head of a dry gill to a ruin where the Old Corpse Road is joined for either a pleasant zigzag descent to the road or an easy way onto the fell top. For a more strenuous day continue into Swindale to the Mosedale Force scramble (Route 110), before crossing the fell again back to Mardale.

109. Guerness Gill

Grade 2★★ NY481134 🔺 🌿

The watercourse is narrow and needs to be fairly dry to enjoy the scrambling to the full. 140m height gain.

The stream runs in a narrow mossy tree-lined ravine which cuts an almost straight trench up the hillside for a considerable distance. There are many cascades, pools and falls which give continuous good sport on rougher rock than is usually encountered hereabouts.

Approach: This is the second gill encountered south of Haweswater Hotel, which lies about halfway along the road overlooking the lake. Just past the gill there is room to park off the road. Enter the stream by the bridge.

Route: The ravine starts almost immediately, and if the first stepped cascade can be climbed by the rocks on its left, then the water level should allow an enjoyable ascent. The main ravine starts above with a delightful succession of little rock steps, pools and cascades in lush vegetated surroundings. The first real hazard is a thin 10m

The waterfall pitch in Guerness Gill

cascade. Climb the steep right wall on shelves with good holds. An innocent-looking mossy slab above on the left proves delicate to surmount. There is easier scrambling for a while, past several trees to a narrowing with a short deep pool. In very dry conditions this could be forced, but usually it is avoided by an ascent of grass ledges on the steep left wall with a traverse back into the ravine above. Pass under a holly and along the side of a pool. The easier gill ends at a sharp left bend where a 12m waterfall is revealed. This makes a fine pitch by a rock groove left of the flow, which is dry in normal conditions. The holds are good, but difficulties will increase if water has to be dealt with. There is an easy escape. A path crosses the stream above, but the ravine continues with good scrambling to pass below a water pipe at its top. The best scrambling ends here, although you can continue further along the diminishing ravine.

SWINDALE

The little valley of Swindale has a pleasing away-from-it-all atmosphere, tucked into a quiet corner of the eastern fells. At one time there were plans to flood the valley, and the waterworks presence is still visible. There are crags with rock climbs, and bird restrictions in season, but the only scramble of worth is the one described.

Car parking
The valley road is narrow and visitors are encouraged to park before Swindale Foot below Bewbarrow Crag. Climbers often drive a further 1km and park on the left just before Truss Gap farm. There is definitely no parking beyond. A pleasant alternative is to approach by mountain bike along the bridleway.

110. Mosedale Force

*Grade 2** NY506116* 🌿🌿

The rock is generally clean but slippery where wet. Best enjoyed in a dry spell. Height gain 100m.

Steep slopes surround Swindale Head where the old pony track zigzags into the boggy upper valley of Mosedale. The main stream cuts through this barrier in a series of cascades. This varied though short trip provides a changing scene of small waterfalls, cascades, deep pools and attractive flora. Although the middle section is bypassed, the rest of the trip is very pleasant.

The rock is generally clean but slippery where wet. Best enjoyed in a dry spell. Height gain 100m.

Approach: Narrow lanes from Bampton Grange or Shap and Rosgill cross the waterworks road and enter the valley. There is ample parking before Swindale Foot. Either follow the narrow valley road to Swindale Head or, before Truss Gap farm, cross a footbridge on the left and take a path which runs below crags on the left side of the valley. A footbridge brings you almost to the start of the scramble at the steep valley head. The scramble is in the main stream left of the pony track.

Route: Keep close to the right edge of the first pool and climb steeply to more gentle terrain. At a wide pool cross the stream and continue by gentle slabs left of the cascade. The rock bed is very wide with plenty of choice. Cross the streambed to gain a clean rib on its left, between the main stream and an overflow channel. For a

*Scrambling in
Mosedale Force*

short distance the stream runs between steep walls. Keep to the rocks, and in reasonably dry weather a not-too-wet way will be found on the right with a slippery exit. The streambed widens again and is crossed to bypass the next fall, but come back into the middle, round the right of a huge boulder to reach a pool above.

The next section appears formidable – a series of small falls between steep rock walls cascade into a deep pool. There is no direct way and the popular solution is to escape by a ledge on the right. (The original way traversed the vegetated left wall, gained through bracken about 10m above the stream, to gain access to the streambed which was crossed to escape on the right wall. This is best left alone.) All this middle section is avoided, although there are some difficult rock traverses and ascents by cascades if you seek them. Regain the stream at a deep pool below a broad waterfall, which is avoided by a detour on the right. The fine fall above has a clean rock stairway on its left, gained by a pool-level traverse. At its top enter a ravine and traverse the left wall on good holds, but as the rocks become wet you made need to finish in stockinged feet.

A return to Truss Gap that incorporates a remote moorland walk can be had by following the path up Mosedale then the old track left towards Wet Sleddale. On the crest go over Scam Matthew and Seat Robert to regain Swindale by a path close to Gouthercrag Gill.

APPENDIX 1
Route Index (alphabetical)

(Note: entries are listed both by scramble route and by crag where appropriate)

Route	Grade	Stars	Page
Ruddy Gill	1 or 2	**	155
Ruthwaite Beck	2	*	209
Sandbed Gill	4	***	179
Scafell, Broad Stand	3	***	83
Scaleclose Gill	1 or 2	*	142
Seathwaite Upper Slabs	1 or 3	*	148
Seavy Knott	3	*	104
Sharp Edge	1	***	197
Shepherd's Crag, Jackdaw Ridge	2	**	136
Skew Gill	1		77
Slab and Notch, Pillar Rock	3	***	92
Sourmilk Gill, Borrowdale	1, 2 or 3	***	146
Sourmilk Gill, Buttermere	2		124
South-West Buttress, Broad Crag	1		82
South-West Buttress, St Sunday Crag	4	*	214
Spout Head Gill	2 or 3	*	74
St Sunday Crag, Broad Buttress	3	**	213
St Sunday Crag, Pinnacle Ridge	3	***	210
St Sunday Crag, South-West Buttress	4	*	214
Stanah Gill	1		185
Stepped Ridge, Brown Cove Crags	2	*	190
Striddle Crag Buttress	4	*	107
Striding Edge	1	***	208
Sulphury Gill	1		232
Swart Beck	3	*	204
Swarthbeck Gill	3		233
Tower Route, Raven Crag	2	*	229
Warnscale Beck	1 or 2	*	108
Westmorland's Crag, Pinnacle Ridge	2	**	69
White Band Crag, Middlefell	2	*	44
White Napes	1		71
Whiteside Gill	1, 2 or 3		188
Windgap Cove, Black Crag, West Buttress	1 or 2		100
Wistow Crags, Pillar	2 or 3	***	59
Yewbarrow, Bell Rib	3	*	52

APPENDIX 2

Route Index (by star grading)

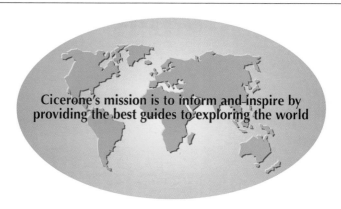

Cicerone's mission is to inform and inspire by providing the best guides to exploring the world

Since its foundation over 30 years ago, Cicerone has specialised in publishing guidebooks and has built a reputation for quality and reliability. It now publishes nearly 300 guides to the major destinations for outdoor enthusiasts, including Europe, UK and the rest of the world.

Written by leading and committed specialists, Cicerone guides are recognised as the most authoritative. They are full of information, maps and illustrations so that the user can plan and complete a successful and safe trip or expedition – be it a long face climb, a walk over Lakeland fells, an alpine traverse, a Himalayan trek or a ramble in the countryside.

With a thorough introduction to assist planning, clear diagrams, maps and colour photographs to illustrate the terrain and route, and accurate and detailed text, Cicerone guides are designed for ease of use and access to the information.

If the facts on the ground change, or there is any aspect of a guide that you think we can improve, we are always delighted to hear from you.

Cicerone Press
2 Police Square Milnthorpe Cumbria LA7 7PY
Tel:01539 562 069 Fax:01539 563 417
e-mail:info@cicerone.co.uk web:www.cicerone.co.uk

CICERONE